BEGINNING AT JERUSALEM

GLENN W. OLSEN

BEGINNING AT JERUSALEM:

*Five Reflections on the History
of the Church*

IGNATIUS PRESS   SAN FRANCISCO

Cover art:
Burial niches with fresco *Christ, ruler of the World* (Pantocrator),
as followed in Byzantine pattern of the 7th or 8th century.
Catacomb of S. Callisto, Rome
Erich Lessing/Art Resource, New York

Cover design by Roxanne Mei Lum

© 2004 Ignatius Press, San Francisco
All rights reserved
ISBN 0–89870–992–x
Library of Congress Control Number 2003115829
Printed in the United States of America ∞

For Suzanne

Et accepit uxorem nomine Susannam, . . .
pulchram nimis et timentem Dominum.
(Daniel 13:2)

CONTENTS

PREFACE

In preparation for the turn to the third millennium, the Wethersfield Institute of the Homeland Foundation in New York
City asked me to direct fifty lectures on Church history to
be given in New York City, ten a year, during the last five
years of the second millennium. I was to divide the history
of the Church into five eras, and nine of the lectures each
year were to present the range of historical developments—
theological, institutional, liturgical—within a single era. The
tenth lecture, however, was to reflect on the significance of
the period, even to draw lessons from it. Though the general
public seems commonly to read its history for the lessons it
might teach, most historians cringe at the suggestion that
their main usefulness is the provision of such lessons, and I
was no exception. As I thought about it, however, a greater
problem emerged: How could I ever find five historical spe-
cialists willing to give such lectures? The answer, partly stemming from despair and partly stemming from the fact that
one does not turn down opportunities to visit New York
lightly, was to offer myself for these five lectures. Thus every
November for five years I traveled to New York to give the
tenth and final lecture on each period, in the process receiv-
ing the splendid hospitality of the Wethersfield Institute, usually offered in person by Msgr. Eugene Clark, now the rector
of Saint Patrick's Cathedral. Subsequently the Institute gave
me permission to publish a revised form of my lectures. These
constitute the five chapters of the present book. The fourth
chapter also contains materials that were given in a lecture in

Ashland, Oregon, in August 1998, on "Thomas More's Anticipation of the Political Dilemmas of Religion in the Modern World", at a Pacific Northwest Honors Conference sponsored by the Intercollegiate Studies Institute.

About the same time I was planning the first of the five lectures for New York City, I was asked to give four lectures on "Prayer in the *Catechism of the Catholic Church*" at the Cathedral of the Madeleine, Salt Lake City. In preparing these I was struck by the *Catechism*'s treatment of the historical dimensions of prayer and subsequently reduced my four lectures to become appendices to the present book, aiming at an exposition of prayer as relation and as Covenant drama. A number of the themes introduced in the five chapters—history as drama, typology, the denial of general progress—are developed in the appendices.

I have incurred many obligations in preparing this work. In addition to Msgr. Clark, special thanks are owed to Msgr. Francis Mannion, rector of the Cathedral of the Madeleine at the time my lectures were given, and to Deacon Owen Cummings, at the time director of religious education at the Cathedral. As always, however, my greatest debt is to my wife, Suzanne. Little did she know, many years ago, that the shared life of *affectio maritalis* would include so much giving of advice on everything from the meaning of Greek and Latin phrases to English usage.

I

Ancient Christianity and Us:
The Once and Future Church [1]

The easy answer to explain the increasing unintelligibility and unfamiliarity of central Christian teachings and practices in our culture is that the age is opposed to them. Schools, parents, and pastors are disinclined to teach them and often themselves lack the education to do so. The more discomfiting answer is that these teachings and practices not only took form in a very different historical situation, but also in important ways depend on that earlier world. This answer implies that our problems are not "merely" doctrinal or moral, but cultural. If this is so, our task must in some degree be recovery of certain habits of being, certain ways of looking at the world, which are not usually perceived as, strictly speaking, at the heart of the Christian faith. That is the argument of the present chapter.

The aim here is to attempt for ancient Christianity something similar to the task Adriaan H. Bredero set himself for the Middle Ages in his book *Christendom and Christianity in*

[1] David Brakke, "The Early Church in North America: Late Antiquity, Theory, and the History of Christianity", *Church History* 71 (2002): 473–91 at 475–80, provides a useful survey of the changing fashions in North America as to how the subject of the present chapter should be understood, as "Church history", "history of Christianity", or "late antiquity".

the Middle Ages. Carl A. Volz described Bredero's book as an attempt "to address the question of the acculturation of Christianity to medieval society and by so doing to raise the further question of how medieval Christianity still is, how much of this tradition is essential, and how much can be discarded".[2] I cannot in one chapter take up all Bredero's questions, which in any case I would reformulate somewhat differently because of my overriding interest in two problems. The first of these is the question of the relevance of ancient Christian developments to our present situation. There is so much that could be said here; there are so many subjects that could be broached! In the interest of economy and clarity, I will let analysis of a single, central question, how the telling of Church history itself passed from its ancient form to become secularized, stand in for dozens of other possible subjects of reflection.

I will follow a three-stage analysis that could be applied to these other subjects. I begin with realization of the inadequacy of modern approaches to this topic, that is, with the unsatisfactoriness of most Church history as now written. From this, in quest of imaginative alternatives, I turn to consideration of ancient approaches to the same topic. In the third stage of analysis I return to the present with alternatives gained from the past and ask how best to present these to a modern audience. Consideration of this one subject will take up most of this chapter, but toward the end I will turn to the second overriding question, already announced: How much of an ancient world view must be retained to keep Christianity intelligible—or rather flourishing—in a mod-

---

[2] Volz's review is found in *Church History* 64 (1995): 280–81. The subtitle of Bredero's book is *The Relations between Religion, Church, and Society*, trans. Reinder Bruinsma (Grand Rapids, Mich.: W. B. Eerdmans, 1994).

ern setting? Here I suggest that central Christian teachings are becoming unintelligible in our world not just because they took form in a very different historical situation, but also because in some important ways they depend on that earlier world. Because, in the spirit of Alasdair MacIntyre, I think we have taken some wrong paths in the modern period, I want to ask whether there is a meaningful sense in which, by retracing our steps, we can find alternatives to what we now have.[3] Clearly we have arrived at some dead ends. The question is whether knowledge of ancient Christianity can still feed our imaginations and suggest alternatives to what we now have.

All history, that of the Church included, has taken place under the sign of contradiction and has been full of irony, tragedy, success that breeds failure, failure unexpectedly successful, roads not taken, and roads taken that should not have been taken. No age has been decisively left behind, and in some sense all earlier ages walk with us. The past provides us with imaginative alternatives to the present, and that which to one age seems dead and decisively left behind appears to another age as something only left in storage, which, retrieved, again seems beautiful. I do not want to make the ancient Church merely into some vast basement from which we may rescue the occasional *objet d'art*, dust it off, and set it again to some useful purpose. Rather, more in the spirit of a great work titled *The World We Have Lost*[4] I want to view ancient Christianity as something with its own integrity and coherence, which can be adequately comprehended only once

---

[3] Entrance to my appropriation of various themes developed by Alasdair MacIntyre may be obtained through my "Why and How to Study the Middle Ages", *Logos: A Journal of Catholic Thought and Culture* 3, no. 3 (2000): 50–75.

[4] Peter Laslett (New York: Scribner, 1971).

we have gained some distance from it, that is, have in some significant measure lost it. There is a sense in which loss of the past is a precondition for its reappropriation. It is only when we have developed a new world, with its own logic and coherence, that we have a contrast by which we can at least in part understand what we have lost. Since this new world is only new, that is, is not necessarily better, comparison of it with what went before can be painful. But the pain of such comparison, sometimes called nostalgia, need not be unproductive. Like an immune system, it can be what preserves a body's health. It locates where disease has entered and may send us looking for a remedy. The more we can compare totalities, the new world won and the old world lost, the more we can see that whatever pains us in the new is likely systemic, something that more needs replacement than repair, a replacement that will have repercussions through the whole. A past age appears less something from which in isolation we can retrieve this or that element than an integrated whole that we may place before our imagination to suggest alternatives to our own times.

The central contrast that appears in a comparison of our age with that of ancient Christianity is this: we have lost God. As the encyclical *Evangelium Vitae* put it:

> We have to go to the heart of the tragedy being experienced by modern man: *the eclipse of the sense of God and of man*, typical of a social and cultural climate dominated by secularism.[5]

John Paul II here was able to identify our central problem because the logic of modern secularism or modernity has

---

[5] John Paul II, *The Gospel of Life, Evangelium Vitae* (Boston: Pauline Books and Media, 1995), no. 21.

worked itself out sufficiently so that we can compare ages. Ours stands revealed as an age in which the sense of God has been eclipsed, and we can now see that because so many of us do not know who God is, we do not know who we are.

As John Paul continued,

"when God is forgotten the creature itself grows unintelligible." Man is no longer able to see himself as "mysteriously different" from other earthly creatures; he regards himself merely as one more living being, as an organism which, at most, has reached a very high stage of perfection. Enclosed in the narrow horizon of his physical nature, he is somehow reduced to being "a thing," and no longer grasps the "transcendent" character of his "existence as man." He no longer considers life as a splendid gift of God, something "sacred" entrusted to his responsibility and thus also to his loving care and "veneration." [6]

This is our situation. We have largely lost the sense of God and therefore do not understand man. Made for a grand end different from that of the other creatures, we have become lost in a nonmysterious, secular order, in which human beings seem no more than possible objects of scientific dissection. We think of ourselves and all other things as mere matter in motion, as *things*, and do not grasp that our primary orientation is as *persons* to God, that is, to transcendence. We can hardly imagine ourselves freed from the confines of immanence and increasingly think of life not as a gift or sacred trust but as something to be manipulated, even reshaped or redefined, by reconfiguring matter. Those of us who remain Christian are filled with a profound uneasiness made possible

[6] Ibid., no. 22.

by being able to compare a culture in which God was at the center with one from which God has largely been removed. We sense that no amount of miscellaneous retrieval of the past will heal our decenteredness.

Our situation would in some ways be easier if the new world were simply systematically in error and could be rejected entirely, were that possible. But in fact the modern world contains great gains as well as losses. To come to terms with it we must engage in a great act of discrimination or discernment. With the goal of separating undesirable from desirable developments, we must examine their interrelations and the possibility of unlinking what history has brought together. For this, contemplation of the past, of previous linkages and ways of seeing things, is invaluable. We have to look backward not so much for specific remedies for various things that have gone astray in our own time, but for another way of looking at the world. Heraclitus once said it is not possible to step into the same stream twice, and we must acknowledge that even the retrieval of a single *object* from the past is not fully possible, for we can never set it again in the setting it formerly had. In this sense the past is past and is dead. What we can do is study first how we became separated from things that seem too valuable for us permanently to have lost and simply now write off, and then how these things worked in their original historical situation. Finally, perhaps in the spirit of Arvo Pärt, John Tavener, or Henryk Górecki, we must perform an act of the imagination and ask what a recovered form of what has been lost—say, the sense of transcendence—could look like in our own historical situation, what form a new transcendence would take.

I cannot detail how we have come to our modern pass and will restrict myself to one subject at the heart of the story of our loss of a sense of God, namely, the secularization of the telling of Church history itself. I need first to sketch quickly how the writing of history, including that of the Church, became secularized, with virtually all sense of mystery and transcendence eliminated. Then I want to suggest that such history has reached a dead end, that is, that the modern period has revealed the incoherence or dishonesty of trying to continue telling one universal story about mankind after either eliminating the premise of such a story, God the author of history, or secularizing this premise into a direction immanent in the historical process itself, usually a form of the idea of progress.[7] That done, I propose, again with John Paul II, but this time following the *Catechism of the Catholic Church*, that we turn to ancient Christianity for better ways of looking at history, which we seem to see now for the first time.

The overall story is well known. According to Genesis, God as the Creator made man as the crowning glory of this world, intended for a great but not fully revealed destiny. History was to be about a cooperation of the human will with God in the pursuit of that destiny, about the forging of a people of God, about a Covenant between God and man. God acted through a series of historical events by which history itself was to be interpreted. The greatest of these was the Incarnation, the life and death of Christ, which most fully revealed what it is to be called to be sons and

---

[7] Glenn Tinder, "The Anti-Gnostic", *First Things*, no. 128 (Dec. 2002): 47–51 at 51, notes that Eric Voegelin, who sought to return political science to religious or transcendental foundations, never finished *Order and History* because he came to think "the past could not be comprehended within a unilinear account." This may be related to the fact that Voegelin held to no institutional form of Christianity and could not affirm that Christian revelation was the ground of history's unity. Without that, Christianity could not be a unilinear tale.

daughters of God. The goal of Church history, that is, of the period after the Ascension of Christ and the coming of the Paraclete, is the spread of this message through all the world and the reshaping of human life according to it. This in a somewhat naive way a great chain of chroniclers of providence, from Eusebius in the fourth century past Bossuet in the seventeenth, tried to narrate.[8] Then in important ways the Age of Reason turned on God and tried to forge a world and a history of the world without him. This was easier said than done, for the Christian narrative had long provided what overall pattern historical narration had. Hardly anyone was up to acknowledging that if God were not the author of history, there would be no reason to believe that history has an author, direction, or point at all, that it would be more than sound and fury signifying nothing. Rather than make such acknowledgment, some made man the sole author of history, and others claimed to discern a kind of secularized or immanent form of providence in the historical process itself. Writer after writer eliminated God from historical narratives, only to conjure up a God-equivalent now called progress instead of providence.[9] For the Hegelian history was written by a spirit immanent in it; for the

---

[8] I have had my say about such views in "Christian Philosophy, Christian History: Parallel Ideas?" presented at a conference, "Catholicism and History", Oxford University, Sept. 6, 1995, and published in a volume issuing from that conference, *Eternity in Time: Christopher Dawson and the Catholic Idea of History*, ed. Stratford Caldecott and John Morrill (Edinburgh: T. and T. Clark, 1997), 131–50 (also to be published in the United States in a book on the theology of history, edited by Warren Carroll and Donald D'Elia).

[9] For both the story and a trenchant classic critique, see the first three chapters of Christopher Dawson, *Progress and Religion*, published in a new edition with a foreword by Christina Scott and an introduction by Mary Douglas (Washington, D.C.: Catholic University of America Press, 2001).

Marxist matter itself was the bearer of a story.[10] But for almost all some form of an idea of progress replaced the old idea of divine providence. One could still take heart from a claimed gradual upward movement or improvement of the race, which seemed to be leading somewhere.

These views became so widespread that many people still hold them, especially in America, the last refuge of the worst ideas of the eighteenth century. One sign of the increasing secularization of Christianity itself was that most Christians came to believe in progress. Certainly such a belief had its critics in great nineteenth-century writers such as Nietzsche and Kierkegaard, and such criticism has continued into the twentieth century with thinkers such as Karl Löwith.[11] Two things have finally come to call progressive beliefs in question for the average man, who often is double-minded and cannot cleanly free himself from their influence: (1) the horrors of the twentieth century, above all the world wars and continuing displacement of peoples, and (2) the inability of liberal societies to solve the great social problems that face them. More and more the historians themselves suspect that history is quirky and unpredictable, not primarily the ineluctable result of powerful economic and social forces, but random.[12]

---

[10] There were differences, as between national traditions, and whereas some of the most prominent exponents of the French Enlightenment tended to view religion simply as superstition, Hegelianism took religion seriously, not thinking that it would be extinguished as life became more modern, but rather that (in a Protestant form) it would provide a kind of "glue" of moral and civic education: Mark Lilla, "A Battle for Religion", *The New York Review of Books* 49, no. 19 (Dec. 5, 2002): 60–65 at 61–62.

[11] *Meaning in History: The Theological Implications of the Philosophy of History* (Chicago: University of Chicago Press, 1949), as all Löwith's books, is still well worth reading.

[12] See the interview by Donald Yerxa, "What Is History Now? An Interview with David Cannadine", *Historically Speaking* 4, no. 3 (Feb. 2003): 4–6

It is increasingly difficult to believe in some general progress of the human race if one cannot find a decent job on graduation from college, if one does not dare walk one's streets at night, or if so-called great powers sometimes seem paralyzed in the face of deep-seated human hatreds and ambition. Thus one of the things that has been revealed by living through the modern period is the emptiness of the attempt to make human life have meaning by transforming the transcendental idea of the divine authorship of history into some immanent secular principle that under the heading of progress preserves a sense of direction but frees us from actually having to cooperate with God. We now have a pretty good sense of what a life constructed on the Enlightenment "in your face" attitude toward God looks like.

We are thus freed to look for some more satisfactory way of thinking about history. This is very difficult, because the presentation of Church history itself has been profoundly influenced by the developments I have just summarized and has become a largely Enlightenment project, in which the tale is told according to the norms of a secularized profession and university, with little suggestion that God might be its author. This must be the subject of another book, and I do not want to be misunderstood, for I think that, as in so many areas, the Enlightenment represents real advance in historical understanding, as well as real loss. I believe that, following Eusebius, many, though not all, historians in the Middle Ages made a serious mistake in writing history as if they knew what was in God's mind and as if they could con-

at 5. See also in the same issue Yerxa's "The Landscape of History: An Interview with John Gaddis", 6–9, with its explanation of why many reductionist theories incorporated into the writing of history from political science have failed to live up to their claims to predictive powers.

fidently chronicle God's judgments in time. Their history had too transcendental a perspective and paid too little attention to intraworldly patterns of causation. In a sense, they called forth the Enlightenment as an inevitable response to such superficiality and arrogance. But here, largely, a facile rationalism replaced a facile providentialism, and in the process a sense of God was lost. Neither form of historical narration adequately understood its own limitations or was able to convey a sense that all history is shrouded in mystery. The narrative techniques of the Enlightenment communicated the idea that the historian confidently can trace progress, but not that we see in a glass darkly. Rare was even a Socratic wisdom, aware that the more we know about the unending complexity of history, the less confident we are of all our patterns and explanations. Instead of a chastened Christian narrative that, while giving up the claim to read the mind of God, continued to affirm that because God is the author of history the historian must tell a story borne of awe and wonder, historical narrative became brisk, confident, rationalistic, matter of fact, and centered solely on intraworldly causal categories rather than the mystery of good and evil and the drama of salvation.[13]

We must relinquish those categories in which Church history, like other forms of history, has been presented as an ongoing tale of progress. One does not have to be a Christian to see this, and my friend Alan Bernstein has written a splendid study, *The Formation of Hell: Death and Retribution in the Ancient and Early Christian Worlds*, which refuses, especially

---

[13] See Olivier Boulnois, "The Concept of God After Theodicy", *Communio: International Catholic Review* 29 (2002): 444–68, esp. 461 and 466–67, for the rejection of progress and the advocacy of drama as a better category for understanding. See also Appendix 2 below.

in its description of Judaism, to present its evidence as pro-
gressing from primitive to more sophisticated views.[14] Bernstein is content to show that the Jews simultaneously affirmed
several different positions, and thus he is faithful to the complexity of the historical record, refusing to bend it to devel-
opmental categories. Would that Christian scholars of the
New Testament, with all their chronologies of the development of this and that, had been equally respectful of that
mysterious figure visible at the center of the text! The critical scholarship of the Enlightenment can tell us many valuable things about this figure, Jesus the Christ, but if it does
not convey the mysteriousness of everything he says and does,
of all the ways in which he does not fit into worldly categories, it fails at the heart of historical narration. It is not that
there is no progress and no development in specific things
such as the spread of the gospel itself or the development of
Christology; it is that history itself has more a dramatic than
a narrative form, the form of permanent struggle more than
the form of any linear story. In it specific instances of progress
and regress are found together, sometimes as two sides of the
same coin. Neither can be eliminated from the historical
record, and therefore history cannot be about one of them
alone, can be neither just about progress nor about decline.

The question, then, if we give up the categories of progress
so dear to the Enlightenment and to the secularization of
historical narration, is with what to replace them. This is the
point at which we turn to the ancient Church for ideas and
alternatives. It seems to me that here we have been anticipated by the author of the fourth part of the *Catechism of the
Catholic Church*. That is, the *Catechism* itself suggests how we

[14] Ithaca, N.Y.: Cornell University Press, 1993.

might turn to the ancient heritage to renew historical narrative.[15] We will pursue this in greater detail in the appendices, but here I wish, in the spirit of the *Catechism*, to do two things: first to show that a number of ancient Christian ways of viewing history are more adequate than ours and then, using the thought of Hans Urs von Balthasar, to show how these ancient views themselves can be deepened.

We must first state that the progressive view of history, which has proved so inadequate, originally formed from separate ideas that, one by one, had truth in them. There clearly is a forward thrust in many biblical texts. The Old Testament calls mankind to great tasks and presents a perspective in which knowledge of God advances, not necessarily in general, but in specific instances. A prophet like Amos, for instance, deepens man's sense of responsibility before God, though the outcome of this is to doubt that more than a remnant of Israel will be saved. Here understanding deepens, but this very advance leads to doubt that it will be received by many. Progress in individual understanding and holiness does not lead to a belief in general progress. So it is in the New Testament. For instance, the prospect for the future given at the end of the Gospel of Luke (24:47, Knox translation) of "repentance and remission of sins ... preached in ... [Christ's] name to all nations, beginning at Jerusalem", implies the preaching of the message of salvation to all mankind, but is open ended as to the reception of this preaching. Luke indeed can elsewhere record Jesus wondering whether he will find any still faithful when he returns. All this should have warned us that legitimate observations, such as that over time the knowledge of God has spread or that God is the caller of men and

---

[15] Throughout I use the 2nd ed., Washington, D.C.: U.S. Catholic Conference—Libreria Editrice Vaticana, 2000.

nations, cannot be knit into an unproblematic progressive narrative. From a Christian point of view, such a perspective conflates things Christianity has always believed in, the hoped-for progress of the individual toward sanctity, the spread of the Church through time, the coming of the Kingdom of God, with something much more problematic, a claimed general and irreversible improvement of the race.

Presumably in response to such distortions, the *Catechism of the Catholic Church*, especially in Part IV on prayer, while retaining the notion of "salvation history", largely abandoned or qualified progressive categories in its own telling of the story of salvation, in the process both recovering ancient Christian ways of viewing the work of God in history, especially under the category of typology, and renewing these views, presumably under the influence of Hans Urs von Balthasar's *Theo-drama*, in which the history of mankind is viewed under the categories of drama.[16] I wish here, in the spirit of the *Catechism*, first to consider how select ancient Christian writers viewed history and then to show how, following von Balthasar, these ancient views can themselves be deepened by bringing them forward into our own times and into dialogue with our problems.

Although views of history are found throughout the New Testament and the earliest postbiblical Christian writings, Christopher Dawson once usefully suggested that the development of Christian theology of history should especially be associated with Irenaeus, bishop of Lyons (c. 130–202).[17] If

---

[16] Subtitle: *Theological Dramatic Theory*, trans. Graham Harrison, 5 vols. (San Francisco: Ignatius Press, 1988–94).

[17] *The Dynamics of World History*, ed. John J. Mulloy (New York: Sheed and Ward, 1956), esp. 233–34. On what follows, see for introduction to Irenaeus, Henry Chadwick, *The Early Church* (Harmondsworth, Middlesex: Penguin

I may explore this in ways that Dawson did not develop, Irenaeus proposed that the history of salvation was a series of recapitulations in which things already known and expressed were returned to and reexpressed in greater depth in later events that in one way or another completed them. Here Irenaeus took up the idea of typology, which had long been developing in both Judaism and Christianity, and gave it his personal impress.[18] Typology expresses the idea that the one God of the universe has been writing into history history's meaning. From a human point of view, this practice originated in Judaism and originally seems, at least in part, to have been a method by which Judaism periodically updated itself, returning to old events to view them anew from some changed historical situation and find in them new meaning. In any case, it was taken over by the Christians and became the principal means by which they affirmed the unity of the

Books, 1967), index under "Irenaeus"; Denis Minns, *Irenaeus* (Washington, D.C.: Georgetown University Press, 1994); Robert M. Grant, *Irenaeus of Lyons* (New York: Routledge, 1997); and Eric Osborn, *Irenaeus of Lyons* (New York: Cambridge University Press, 2001).

[18] See Glenn W. Olsen, "Allegory, Typology and Symbol: The *Sensus Spiritalis*, Part I: Definitions and Earliest History", *Communio* 4 (1977): 161–79, "Part II: Early Church through Origen", ibid., 257–84. The first two volumes of Henri de Lubac's great work on the subject have now been translated as *Medieval Exegesis*, vols. 1–2: *The Four Senses of Scripture*, vol. 1, trans. Mark Sebanc, vol. 2, trans. E. M. Macierowski (Grand Rapids, Mich.: W. B. Eerdmans, 1998–2000). For the current state of debate, see John David Dawson, *Christian Figural Reading and the Fashioning of Identity* (Berkeley, Calif.: University of California Press, 2002), with the review of Joseph W. Trigg, *Journal of Early Christian Studies* 10 (2002): 524–26, and for the Middle Ages, Gilbert Dahan, *L'exégèse chrétienne de la Bible en Occident médiéval: XII–XIVe siècle* (Paris: Cerf, 1999), with the review by E. Ann Matter, *Speculum* 77 (2002): 1272–74; and Jane Dammen Mcauliffe, Barry D. Walfish, and Joseph W. Goerring, eds., *With Reverence for the Word: Medieval Scriptural Exegesis in Judaism, Christianity, and Islam* (New York: Oxford University Press, 2003).

Old and New Covenants. God had written history in such a way that great events in the Jewish Scriptures, called types, were linked to, and looked forward to their completion in, later events, called antitypes, associated with the coming of Christ as the Messiah, who fulfilled Jewish expectation. The movement of history was from Shadow to Image to Reality, from things less clearly seen to things more clearly seen.[19] The bronze serpent raised in the wilderness was in its time an instrument of healing, but in God's plan also looked forward to and anticipated the raising of Christ on the Cross for the healing of the race. Joseph Cardinal Ratzinger has suggested that in such a schema the time of the New Testament, the Church, and the liturgy is a kind of in-between time, caught between Shadow and Reality, between "already" and "not yet".[20] We see enough to know that we stand in the history of salvation. With Christ we have moved from the shadow of Jewish history to Image, preserved in the liturgy, but we do not fully see the Reality that is still to be.

Irenaeus saw recapitulation in its narrowest and most specific sense to lie in a correspondence or parallelism between Adam and Christ. Paul had spoken of the first and second Adams, each of whom stood for the entire race. By the first Adam, all had fallen. By the second Adam, Christ, all had been offered salvation. Adam was the first of men, Christ the first of the new men. The New Covenant recapitulates

---

[19] The classic study here is Jean Daniélou, *From Shadows to Reality: Studies in the Biblical Typology of the Fathers*, trans. Wulstan Hibberd (Westminster, Md.: Newman Press, 1960).

[20] *The Spirit of the Liturgy*, trans. John Saward (San Francisco: Ignatius Press, 2000), esp. 53–61. See also the entry by T. A. Friedrichsen on "Time" with a subsection on "Time (in the New Testament)" in *New Catholic Encyclopedia*, 2nd ed. Berard L. Marthaler (New York: Catholic University of America Press, 2003), vol. 14, 77–84.

the original creation. Christ's humanity is that which Adam possessed before the fall. When Adam sinned, he remained in God's image but lost similitude to God. Through Christ mankind may regain this similitude, that is, not just have Godlike capacities, but regain similitude by actually doing God's will and thus using God-given capacities for the purposes for which they had originally been intended. In sum, for Irenaeus salvation was a restoration to man of Adam's state before the fall. Adam was a kind of immature child destined for a great end who early on made the mistake of disobedience and thus thwarted his destiny. With the coming of Christ mankind may again take up Adam's task and move to a fuller maturity. To quote Irenaeus' famous phrase: "The glory of God is man fully alive."[21] History is thus a process by which man has been educated, has been allowed to make mistakes and learn discipline. We note in this that Irenaeus, by comparing history and education, has at one and the same time been able to articulate a sense in which there is development in history, but also fall, reversal, recovery, and possibly the regaining of paths earlier lost, to advance on them to no known end. History is not so much progressive as open ended or indeterminate.

Origen, the greatest Christian thinker of the third century, saw the possibilities of the perspectives Irenaeus had opened. For Origen the great problem was how to reconcile God's goodness with human freedom. If God is good, then although for the sake of freedom he might allow evil ("not good" or "less than the best") temporarily, it does not seem

---

[21] *Adv. Haers.* 4, 20, 7, quoted in *Catechism of the Catholic Church*, 294. See also Y. de Andia, *Homo uiuens. Incorruptibilité et divinisation de l'homme chez Irénée de Lyon* (Paris: Études augustiniennes, 1986), and John Behr, *Asceticism and Anthropology in Irenaeus and Clement* (New York: Oxford University Press, 2000).

that God could be God and allow evil finally to prevail. It would seem that if God is God, in the end there must be only good. Yet the very concept of human freedom seems to involve being able to resist God to the end, that is, seems to involve the possibility of unrepentant evil with no limit. With the author of the Fourth Gospel, we must hope that all men will be saved and that eventually all creatures will choose to do God's will, but it is unclear from our experience that this can be so. Thus Origen ends with a question that has made him the target of much criticism. If God is God, then how can anyone, the devil included, finally be given up on as irredeemable? But if man is free, how can God's will prevail in the end? My purpose here is not to pursue that great question, "May we hope that all men will be saved?" further, but to note that by resisting easy answers Origen has wonderfully expanded the sense in which history is educational.[22] He rules out either a prematurely closed belief in God's final victory or a prematurely closed despair over human evil. What history offers is a stage on which, stretching as far forward as does hope itself, the drama of salvation is being worked out, a drama that involves as a limit a perfect healing of the human will in which men would freely do what God wills of them and thus could in a sense themselves be spoken of as divinized.[23]

There is a sense in which in the thought of both Irenaeus and Origen the end is like, or is meant to be like, the be-

[22] The themes involved here are the subject of many of the writings of Hans Urs von Balthasar: see for a summary treatment his *Dare We Hope "That All Men Be Saved"? With a Short Discourse on Hell*, trans. David Kipp and Lothar Krauth (San Francisco: Ignatius Press, 1988). Cf. Georgios Lekkas, *Liberté et progrès chez Origène* (Turnhout, Belgium: Brepols, 2001).

[23] See further my "Problems with the Contrast between Circular and Linear Views of Time in the Interpretation of Ancient and Early Medieval History", *Fides quaerens intellectum* 1 (2001): 41–65.

ginning. That is, just as Irenaeus sees in Christ's humanity and in the new men who are imitators of Jesus Christ the recapturing of Adam's condition before the fall, Origen sees the recovery of likeness to God that a restored will makes possible as a kind of return of the soul to the state in which it was before it entered its human body. If we move down in time another century to another Greek Christian Father, Gregory of Nyssa, we find this perspective broadened into an even more sweeping idea of Christian reform. Gregory insists that the end is more, in fact infinitely more, than the beginning.[24] He suggests that we are made forever to move "from glory to glory". That is, since we are finite and God is infinite, we may become, in this life and the next, ever more like him without becoming him. Origen had already suggested that there is no reason to believe that the hoped-for ever-more-perfect imitation of the Creator by the creature ends with death or the end of history. Gregory takes up this idea to argue that while life in history is supposed to be about ever-increasing recovery of likeness to God, that is, about sanctification without limit, there is no reason to limit

---

[24] The issues are treated in much more detail than can be given here in Gerhart Ladner, *The Idea of Reform: Its Impact on Christian Thought in the Age of the Fathers*, rev. ed. (New York: Harper and Row, 1967). See also Jaroslav Pelikan, *Christianity and Classical Culture: The Metamorphosis of Natural Theology in the Christian Encounter with Hellenism* (New Haven, Conn.: Yale University Press, 1993); Hans Urs von Balthasar, *Presence and Thought: An Essay on the Religious Philosophy of Gregory of Nyssa*, trans. Mark Sebanc (San Francisco: Ignatius Press, 1995); and Brian E. Daley, "Training for 'the Good Ascent': Gregory of Nyssa's Homily on the Sixth Psalm", in *In Dominico Eloquio—In Lordly Eloquence: Essays on Patristic Exegesis in Honor of Robert Louis Wilken*, ed. Paul M. Blowers et al. (Grand Rapids, Mich.: W.B. Eerdmans, 2002), 185–217, and " 'Heavenly Man' and 'Eternal Christ': Apollinarius and Gregory of Nyssa on the Personal Identity of the Savior", *Journal of Early Christian Studies* 10 (2002):469–88.

this dynamic to life here below. He sees the restless and un-
fulfilled encounters of the Song of Songs, in which the bride
never quite grasps the Divine Lover, as illustrative of the endless pursuit of God in which the Christian will forever be
engaged. In his twelfth homily on the Song of Songs, Gregory says of the bride:[25]

> But when, like Moses, she hoped that the face of the King
> would be made visible to her, her *beloved turned aside* (Cant.
> 5.6) from her comprehension. Thus she says: *My beloved turned
> aside*—but this was not with the intention of abandoning the
> soul that followed Him, but rather to draw her to Himself.

Gregory speculatively presents the next life as centered on
unending increasing likeness to God.

It seems to me that Gregory of Nyssa's view of unlimited
spiritual progress is much more satisfactory than modern progressive views on two scores. Precisely because, with his predecessors and with Augustine in the West, Gregory sees
progress toward sanctity as above all the work of individuals,
one by one, Gregory's idea of the call to ever-greater perfection in time never translates into belief that there is general progress in time. Secondly, although only speculatively,
he suggests a perspective in which history itself becomes
dwarfed by a much larger tale. History is deeply mysterious
for Gregory because it is but one part of a much larger dynamic. More insistently than any earlier writer, Gregory believes that what we begin in time flourishes in eternity, that
what is done in time leads to an everlasting life of progress
Godward. Either insight would have prevented the develop-

---

[25] Jean Daniélou, *From Glory to Glory: Texts from Gregory of Nyssa's Mystical
Writings*, trans. Herbert Musurillo (New York: Scribner, 1961), 261. Daniélou's
introduction provides excellent orientation to Gregory.

ment of the modern forms of historical narrative, from which are absent Gregory's sense of the possibilities history opens up and the corresponding mystery within which we walk every day of our life.

Although the thought of Gregory's contemporary, Augustine, is much better known than that of his Greek Christian predecessors and contemporaries, it is nevertheless to the point to note its relevance to this analysis. In his thirties Augustine dreamed Eusebian dreams. With most of his contemporaries, he accepted the coming together of Christianity with longstanding pagan hope for, in Virgil's words (*Aeneid*, I, line 278), an empire that would know "no bounds in space or time". That is, Augustine initially hoped for a universal unending political order, an eternal Rome, now in the form of the Christian Roman Empire. This had apparently been established by the Christian emperors from Constantine to Theodosius. Augustine's initial instinct had been Eusebian, that is, to hail the work of providence that had merged Christianity and the empire in the person of Constantine. On reflection, however, he came to see all history, as well as the Church, as mixed, that is, as composed of an intermingling of good and evil that would never be separated until the Last Judgment. Once the biblical record of God's saving events closed, that is, in any period subsequent to the New Testament record, we have no special access to God's mind to allow us to explain the course of the providence we do believe to be at work. *Pace* all the medieval cries that "God wills it" in regard to this or that battle, God does not seem to act so partisanly, so unequivocally, through one or the other historical institution that we can without reservation declare it the will of God. One can reasonably wonder about, say, the placing of saints in service to national aspiration, as in the case of Joan of Arc, even when the logic of accepting the saint's claim at all seems to involve that one knows which side God was on in 1430.

The Church herself has many in her who do not do God's will. Thus Augustine declares, "We are the times: such as we are, such are the times." [26] That is, on the one hand the Greek Fathers were right to see that sanctification of the individual is central to any progress made in history: the condition of any age is the sum of individual movements to or away from God. On the other hand, many of the Greek Fathers too easily, in the wake of Constantine's conversion, made history less problematic than it is by accepting the idea that the Constantinian settlement represented a real general advance for mankind. For Augustine, because God writes history, it will always be problematic, a puzzle and a mystery, to men.

With Augustine we near the end and summit of ancient Christianity. It was by going back to the period we have just traversed that the *Catechism* renewed a Christian view of history as an alternative to all progressive accounts. But the *Catechism* did more than retrieve the past. In trying to present Catholicism to the contemporary world, it both took stock of that world and tried to present ancient views in a way that really would renew. Thus, on the one hand, the fourth part of the *Catechism*, devoted to the subject of prayer, is full of typological perspectives, some of them very adventuresome. But the *Catechism* did more than present the historical development of prayer typologically. The *Catechism* cast about for a historical framework centered on ancient typology but also informed of recent work in the theology of history. Although his name is never mentioned, it seems quite clear,

---

[26] *Sermon* 80, quoted in R. A. Markus, *Saeculum: History and Society in the Theology of St. Augustine*, rev. ed. (Cambridge, Eng.: Cambridge University Press, 1988), 40–41.

especially in sections that speak of history as drama, that behind the thought of this part of the *Catechism* lies that of Hans Urs von Balthasar. That is, the *Catechism* sees that von Balthasar's earlier attack on progressive historical accounts and development of a dramatic alternative to them are a most compelling way in which to set the work of the ancient thinkers to new uses. The *Catechism* retains such expressions as "salvation history", but to them ties a language taken from the stage, from plays and drama.

The argument is that what we have been calling history is best viewed as a sequence of dramas or dramatic moments, in which the story of redemption, of sin and grace, keeps getting worked out with various scripts, actors, and settings. God is the author of the drama in which we are actors; we have received a script about which, within limits, we can negotiate with the Author; and each time this drama is recounted, some particular truth is highlighted, probably some truth is obscured. Thus no repeat of the drama definitively dates the others: all retain their value. Most striking of all, with Christ the Author has stepped on the stage and revealed to us an order that redefines beauty as we formerly understood it, teaching us that the first will be last, the humble exalted, and that he who loses his life will gain it.

Thus the story of salvation presented in the *Catechism* is as much drama as narrative, full of surprises, twists, reversals, and fulfillments. It is not a smooth narrative of upward advance, but one radically open to the drama of salvation as worked out by saint and sinner. As Josef Pieper insisted, freedom and mystery are central to being in history.[27] As with ancient plays, resolutions never lose their relevance, but retain

---

[27] *The End of Time: A Meditation on the Philosophy of History*, trans. Michael Bullock (San Francisco: Ignatius Press, 1999). Unfortunately, Pieper's book

an everlasting truth. Job's struggles with the problems of suffering and justice are not somehow outmoded by what the Evangelist John has to say, but resonate within and with later dramatic attempts to script all that must be said of these subjects.

The view I would advance here is that because, more than a progressive narrative, Church history is ongoing drama, ever scripting anew the struggle between sin and grace and open to radical good and radical evil, enlightenment and degradation, the perspectives of ancient Christianity are eternally relevant. If we wish a world from which God has not been removed, nor our sense of him diminished, we must reappropriate ancient perspectives. This does not merely mean that typology will never lose its appropriateness as a vehicle to tell the story of salvation as authored by God. Leopold Von Ranke grasped an important truth when he suggested that each age is equally under the eye of God. We may give a von Balthasarian cast to this observation by saying that each age is directly under the eye of God in that it has its own ways of living out the drama of salvation, with resolutions that remain for us to reappropriate as our situation demands.

The second problem announced for brief analysis at the beginning of this chapter was the question how much of an ancient world view must be retained to keep Christianity intelligible in a modern setting. This large question can be considered by looking at one central problem, how we are to keep intelligible the communal, communitarian, or non-individualist nature of ancient Christian thought, which framed the development of central doctrines. This question is closely related to the analysis thus far. To recapitulate,

contains the simplifications about circular views of time criticized in my "Problems with the Contrast between Circular and Linear Views of Time".

Irenaeus affirmed a typological connection between Adam and Christ. In this both Adams stood for mankind. Such a form of thought is very difficult for someone from an individualistic culture such as ours to appreciate, but also, I would argue, necessary to retain if we are to retain Christianity itself. For if, because of our individualism, it becomes impossible for us to think in terms of what the Stoics called universal particulars, in our case one man standing for all men, much of the essence of ancient Christianity will be lost to us. We will be unable to give any convincing account of how we have all inherited Adam's sin or of how we have all been restored in Christ.

Many contemporary assumptions make it very difficult to appreciate the central Christian doctrines of the Trinity, original sin, redemption through the saving act of Christ, baptism, the Eucharist, and the communion of saints. In each case, the individualism of a noncontemplative society stands between us and appropriation of these doctrines. Our society teaches us that the individual is its basic unit, and we have become so used to the assumption that the individual is a kind of ultimate reality, autonomous and atomistic, that we have become psychologically removed from earlier points of view, which always saw the individual as defined by something larger, a family, tribe, or city, by being born into some form of relationship. Again, we instinctively think of this individual as active and busy, not as first of all made for contemplation, that is, to be receptive before being in all its forms. I think our point of view here is simply wrong and indefensible. The very idea of the individual is comprehensible only in relation to something else, some form of community. It is not just that what I will call the *communio* perspectives of ancient Christianity, both social and contemplative, can instruct us as to mistaken ideas we have become used to. It is literally that without abandonment of these contemporary ideas we can hardly understand what we are about, let alone what Christianity is about. That is the real meaning of John Paul's frightening words that in losing the sense of God we have lost a sense of ourselves.

The point can be made in regard to infant baptism. Presumably the earliest Christians were mostly baptized as adults, for the simple reason that they converted to Christianity as adults. By the time of Augustine, increasingly baptism was of infants. This is easy enough to explain socially, for over the generations more and more babies were born into already existing Christian families. But what made the idea of "cradle Catholicism", that is, of baptizing babies before they could choose the faith for themselves, acceptable? Presumably it was the same thing that made original sin intelligible, or indeed the idea that either Adam or Christ could stand in for the whole race. One never thought of oneself as definable or in a certain sense existing except in a group. People thought more of themselves as defined into existence by a group than as choosing a life. Thus what was central was that the baby be baptized into a Christian family, or into the Christian Church, because those were the communities from which, so to speak, one received one's marching orders.

Corporate thought was natural, and so one could speak of belonging to the Body of Christ. It is not that no individualism was present, but that always the larger horizon was some form of human society. Without this, the ideas of the communion of saints, or indeed of Eucharistic Communion itself, lose their plausibility. Much of Protestantism, especially the Calvinist branches, are witness to this.[28] If the

---

[28] One could use the history of confirmation to show all the tensions leading toward Calvinism by a kind of internal logic in high medieval reform

ultimate reality is the individual, then the logic is against the Real Presence, against infant baptism, and against the communion of saints. We stand in splendid isolation as choosing beings. Even a pagan such as Aristotle could see that the human soul is in some sense permeable, capable for instance of uniting with the object of its contemplation. In some manner the individual is capable of coinherence in another. That is, Aristotle could see a sense in which, friend with friend or man with wife, we become the other, coinhere in another. For him as many ancients, there is a sense in which "you are me", and "I am you." The ancient Christians expressed this in the idea that the married couple must seek each other's salvation, that likely they would find salvation together or not at all. Such a background is necessary to appreciate much of Christian theology. Again the Neoplatonists expressed the idea that sometimes in this life we "pass yonder". That is, the self "disappears", and we become aware of this only when we return to ourselves. When they said this the Neoplatonists had contemplation in mind, in which we pass over to union with the thing contemplated, but what they were speaking of is open to moderns and has its analogue, for instance, in becoming lost at a concert, lost in or united with the music. My point is that without such categories we will be unable to

---

thought, with its concern with proper instruction and conscious decision, that is, "rational" and "individualistic" categories that found the cosmic and communitarian categories of ancient Christianity one-sided and inadequate. From the high Middle Ages there was a tendency for cosmic and liturgical perspectives to fall by the wayside when the attention focused on rational and educative categories. See Nicholas Orme, *Medieval Children* (New Haven, Conn.: Yale University Press, 2001) on twelfth- and thirteenth-century educational developments: in treating the sacraments, theologians increasingly stressed the difference between children and adults.

appreciate much that is Christian, from the ordering categories of prayer to trinitarianism itself.

Our work is cut out for us. To be ignorant of ancient Christianity is to be unaware of ways out of modern dead ends, to be impoverished in our imaginations, to be unable to make the comparisons that could lead to critical assessment of our own assumptions, and to leave much of the doctrinal heritage of Christianity a largely closed book. *Evangelium Vitae* reminded us of the great destiny of the human race, shrouded in mystery but glorious in goal. In words that recall the Fathers at every step, the Pope quotes Paul's letter to the Romans to describe the race as "Called . . . to be conformed to the image of his Son"[29] and reminded us that "God's glory shines on the face of man."[30] We are "*a manifestation of God in the world, a sign of his presence, a trace of his glory*".[31] These words reexpress for our times an ancient Christian sense of participation in a great human destiny being worked out in mystery and struggle. They are rooted in an attention to the ancient Church that we might well emulate.

---

[29] Romans 8:28–29, quoted in *Evangelium Vitae*, title to no. 34.

[30] *Evangelium Vitae*, title to no. 34.

[31] Ibid., no. 34; see Gen 1:26–27; Ps 8:6.

II

Late Ancient and Early Medieval Christianity:
A World We Have Lost?

The world of late ancient and early medieval Christianity seems so obviously remote from ours, so obviously lost to us, that it hardly occurs to us that we might sit at its feet and learn. "What has a world overrun by barbarians in which illiteracy seems to increase daily have to do with us?" we ask, only to have the question freeze in our throats. In fact, I could devote this chapter to pursuing the many parallels that exist between those and our times. My goal lies elsewhere and is, rather, to show how important for our own day is knowledge of the discoveries and developments of the late antique and early medieval world.

In attacking an ecclesiastical form of primitivism, what he called "chronological snobbery", that is, a preference for or privileging of primitive Christianity over all subsequent development, C. S. Lewis famously described the history or development of the Church as similar to that of an onion, each period, so to speak, becoming a new layer. If, under the assumption that the best was at the beginning, one attempts to peel through the accrued layers in search of the purported pure and perfect beginnings beyond which all development was distortion or decline, one ends up destroying the onion. We feel the force of this analogy when we ourselves want to retain the achievements of one of the layers of historical development, perhaps some favored period in the history of art or music with which we ourselves identify. But who speaks for the early Middle Ages? Who defends that layer of the onion? Who speculates about how its existence was one of God's gifts, without which we would be the poorer?

In the twentieth century primitivism was an occupational weakness of students of the liturgy, and especially many of the great liturgists of the twentieth century have taught us to despise the loss of the primitive or patristic liturgy and shape of things during the Middle Ages. The single most influential historian of the liturgy in the twentieth century, Josef Jungmann, presented the history of the development of the medieval liturgy as, in Eamon Duffy's words, a "story of decline from the true liturgical participation of all the people during the patristic age, to subjective and uncomprehending pietism in the later Middle Ages".[1] In his *The Stripping of the Altars*, Duffy has masterfully refuted such a perspective for the late Middle Ages.[2] I cannot in one chapter equal this achievement for the early Middle Ages, partly because the

[1] Fredric M. Roberts, "The Stripping of the Altars and the Liturgy: Some Reflections on a Modern Dilemma" (Overview of Keynote Address of the Same Title Given at the Conference "Catholic Liturgy Thirty Years After Vatican II", September 1995, Salt Lake City, by Eamon Duffy), *Antiphon: Publication of the Society for Catholic Liturgy* 1, no. 1 (Spring 1996): 2–4 at 2. Theodor Klauser, *A Short History of the Western Liturgy: An Account and Some Reflections*, trans. John Halliburton, 2nd ed. (Oxford: Oxford University Press, 1979), schematizes the history of the liturgy in a way similar to Jungmann: we move from the ideal liturgy of the early Church, degraded in the Middle Ages and virtually lost in the Tridentine reforms, to recovery with Vatican II of the first rites. For orientation see further Paul F. Bradshaw, *The Search for the Origins of Christian Worship: Sources and Methods for the Study of Christian Worship* (New York: Oxford University Press, 1993).

[2] New Haven, Conn.: Yale University Press, 1992.

periods are so different and partly because I do not want to restrict myself to the liturgy, but I would like to attempt something with some parallels.

I want to take a list of developments specific to the late Roman and early medieval Church, developments that I think one can safely say are unknown, neglected, or looked upon with condescension by most modern people, Christians or not, and show not just the intrinsic importance of these developments, but how impoverished we are without them, how they might continue to "speak to us". By conventional standards, the list is most unpromising: it is composed of (1) angels and, because where angels are found he cannot be far away; (2) Pseudo-Dionysius the Areopagite; (3) the cult of the saints; (4) the communion of saints; and (5) the liturgical developments that Jungmann most regretted. These represent a "world we have lost", but also a world, the argument is, that still lies open to our hollowness and poverty of imagination.

By consideration of the subjects in this list, I want us to unlearn interpretive perspectives on the early medieval world that our contemporaries have inculcated in us. Let me begin with the angels.[3] Today there is considerable fascination with the subject of angels, and we come across these spiritual beings who mediate between heaven and earth in a variety of movies, stories, reproductions, and artwork. One might almost think that the natural habitat of the angel is the

[3] I am very grateful to Deacon Owen Cummings for having made available to me the text of a lecture he delivered in Salt Lake City, May 19, 1996, "Do Angels Exist?" I am heavily indebted to this paper for the following discussion of the angels. See also David Keck, *Angels and Angelology in the Middle Ages* (New York: Oxford University Press, 1998), and *Angelic Spirituality: Medieval Perspectives on the Ways of Angels*, trans. Steven Chase, preface Ewert H. Cousins (New York: Paulist Press, 2002).

gift shop. Yet, though angelic beings have been believed in across the ages, one guesses that much of current fascination with them is more related to dabbling in the esoteric than to any serious understanding of the angels' role in historic Christianity. Certainly renewed interest in the angels may signal rejection of a narrow and rationalistic view of reality, which we have inherited from thinkers such as Descartes and Newton, and willingness to consider some postmodern view of the world more characterized by openness and receptivity.[4] Still, it seems fair to say that at any serious level the angels are more disbelieved in than believed in and that for the most part they are simply ignored and seen as irrelevant to the world as it is, indeed, to Christianity itself.

It was not always so. The angels had a particularly prominent place in late Roman and early medieval Christianity. Around the year 600 Pope Gregory the Great, in describing the Eucharist, declared, "For, who of the faithful can have any doubt that at the moment of the sacrifice, at the sound of the priest's voice, the heavens stand open and choirs of angels are present at the mystery of Jesus Christ. There at the altar the lowliest is united with the most sublime, earth is joined to heaven, the visible and invisible somehow merge into one." [5] In Gregory's earth- and heaven-connecting vision, the celebration of the Eucharist is as much something done in heaven as on earth, a shared action or communion between earth and heaven. At the moment of Eucharistic Consecration, the heavens open, and we see that what we

---

[4] See Seyyed Hossein Nasr, *Religion and the Order of Nature* (Oxford: Oxford University Press, 1996).

[5] I have slightly altered the translation of *Dialogues* 4.60.3, of Odo Zimmerman, *Saint Gregory the Great, Dialogues* (Fathers of the Church, vol. 39; New York: Fathers of the Church, 1959), 273.

are doing is the same thing that the angels perpetually do and that we are doing it with them. Our Sacrifice and theirs are the same. We also see that we are not alone in the universe, that being is much fuller than we might have expected. We are part of some vast communion, some vast song in praise of the Creator.

I want to approach Gregory's breathtaking vision from a couple of angles. First, today we live in a world that has been largely denuded by science and technology of everything that in past times connected it to the heavens. This has been through a series of improper conclusions drawn from developments that in other ways command our respect. One of the results of the redefinition of the natural order according to the criteria of mathematics from the time of Newton is the widely accepted notion of "dead matter". That is, matter has come to be defined according to the interests of the physicist as that which is measurable, and reality itself has tended to be conceived as no more than "matter in motion". This is the conception at the base of other modern ideas such as the promise of science to give power over the world, with the related view of nature as so much raw material to be used by man as he wills.

The inadequacy of such notions, which have dominated the last three hundred years, has begun to be seen today, for instance, in some forms of the ecological movement, but even Christians have largely forgotten what a more thoroughly Christian view of nature would look like. Virtually no one beyond a few Orthodox writers speaks of the cosmos as itself involved, along with man, in both Fall and Redemption.[6] The Gospel of John declares that God is love, and one

---

[6] See however Glenn W. Olsen, "The Role of Religion in the Twenty-First Century: Epoch of Secularization or Cosmos Regained?" *Actas del VII*

of the great labors of late Roman and early medieval thought
was to articulate the idea that love is the form of the world.
That is, if seen from above, from the viewpoint of revelation, everything in the world bears the mark of love, including matter itself. There is no such thing as dead matter, and
no possibility of properly reducing the world to being no
more than matter in motion. In a Christian universe all things,
including those that lack reason and will, are in some way
ordered to God, are teleological.[7]

Belief in the angels did not simply reinforce the view that,
seen from above, the world is in its highest aspects spiritual;
it presented the visible and material as connected to and in
some sense supporting and opening to things higher than
itself. Certain of the Church Fathers spoke of the body as, in
a holy face or an august bearing, capable of expressing a proper
notion of matter in service to soul or spirit, and the various
Neoplatonisms of the late Fathers and early Middle Ages saw
in symbol, especially in icons, something transcendant, a window on eternity.[8] Sacramental theory itself from the time of
Augustine stressed that sacraments participate in a reality
higher than themselves. The point is that, in the early Middle Ages, the angels stood as the capstone in a view of the

---

Congreso "Cultura Europea", ed. Enrique Banús and Beatriz Elío (Pamplona,
scheduled for 2004 publication; also in Poland in *The Quarterly of Architecture
and Urban Planning* [Warsaw] and in the U.S. in the *Catholic Social Science Review* 8 [2003]: 183–205) on such thinkers as Peter Casarella.

[7] For orientation see *Beyond Mechanism: The Universe in Recent Physics and
Catholic Thought*, ed. David L. Schindler (Lanham, Md.: University Press of
America, 1986), and Schindler's subsequent *Heart of the World, Center of the
Church: Communio Ecclesiology, Liberalism, and Liberation* (Grand Rapids, Mich.:
W. B. Eerdmans, 1996).

[8] Of a series of articles in which I have been analyzing such texts, I note
"Twelfth-Century Humanism Reconsidered: The Case of St. Bernard", *Studi
Medievali*, 3a Serie, 31, no. 1 (1990): 27–53.

world that stressed the closeness of this world and the next and the many ways in which what is done here below is linked to eternity. Early medieval people faced many material and physical difficulties, but they were not isolated from the world in ways that we are; they were not "lost in the cosmos". The angels stand to remind us that there is a better way to talk of the plenitude of being than to accept the notion of "dead matter" as the last word in how we imagine the material order.

This plenitude of being needs more attention, for it gives a second angle on the angels. Angelology has always affirmed a plenitude of being, that God is prolific in his creation, and that more species than ourselves inhabit the cosmos. Thus the theologian John Macquarrie has written,

> Man is sometimes afflicted with a sense of loneliness on his little planet, the only "existent" upon earth, perhaps just an accident in the cosmos. But if the Christian doctrine of creation is true, then man is no accident, and presumably he is not alone.... The doctrine of the angels opens our eyes to this vast, unimaginable cooperative striving and service, as all things seek to be like God and to attain fullness of being in him.... The panorama of creation must be far more breathtaking than we can guess in our corner of the cosmos.[9]

The doctrine of the angels expresses the glory, mystery, and fullness of the universe.

[9] John Macquarrie, *Principles of Christian Theology*, 2nd ed. (London: Scribner, 1977), 234–37, quoted by Cummings. Cf. the very striking and original attack on various relativist ideas that deny the centrality of human history by John Lukacs, *At the End of an Age* (New Haven, Conn.: Yale University Press, 2002), and the more explicitly theological Michael Schulz, " 'Fallen' Nature: How Sin Affects the Creation", *Communio* 29 (2002): 490–505 at 497–99.

When many churches in the wake of Vatican II were at
least metaphorically whitewashed and stripped of, among
other things, their angels, it was as if these now barren
churches finally visually came into line with or expressed the
emptiness of the universe according to the scientific view
that I have mentioned. As is so often the case, the irony was
that the science underlying such a view had increasingly become dated. Nevertheless, the angels took it in the neck.
Bernard Cooke, in a kind of parody of the Council of Trent,
said that since we have Christ, we have no need of the angels, particularly guardian angels. Such positions seem to me
mean spirited, to hide the nature of God's bounty. In the
high Middle Ages Saint Thomas Aquinas responded to the
question "whether God wills things other than himself?" by
linking God and the idea that goodness is diffusive of itself:
"If natural things, in so far as they are perfect, communicate
their good to others, much more does it pertain to the divine will to communicate by likeness its own good to others
as much as is possible. Thus, then, He wills both Himself to
be, and other things to be." [10] This is the best statement of
why angels exist. God wishes to share his goodness and gifts.
One may hope that others follow the lead of Msgr. Francis
Mannion in preserving the angels in the restoration of the
Cathedral of the Madeleine in which I worship in Salt Lake
City. This restored cathedral is full of angels. Especially striking, in relation to the text from Gregory the Great with which
we began, are eight great angels painted on the ceiling at the
transept crossing above the altar. It is difficult to worship in
this church without being reminded of the company of the
angels, that God has been much more prolific in his dealing

[10] *ST*, I, 19, 2, *Ad Resp.*, trans. Anton C. Pegis, *Basic Writings of Saint
Thomas Aquinas*, 2 vols. (New York: Random House, 1945), vol. 1, 197.

with the universe than early modern science suggested. In the book of Revelation, a special favorite of the writers of the early Middle Ages, the heavenly hosts are described as bringing time and creation in the New Jerusalem to their fulfillment. Every person who enters the cathedral in Salt Lake City is reminded of such a perspective, and this church stands as an alternative to our current impoverishment in matters liturgical and architectural.

I stated earlier that where we find the angels, Pseudo-Dionysius the Areopagite cannot be far away, and with that observation I move to my second topic.[11] We call him *Pseudo-Dionysius* because, other than knowing that he was a mystical writer of the sixth century, we know virtually nothing about Dionysius beyond that he carried the name of that Denys of whom the Scripture speaks (Acts 17:34), who was converted on the Areopagus by Saint Paul. Dionysius or Denys is the writer who has had the greatest influence until the present in defining the order or ranks of the angels. From the Old Testament he took the cherubim and seraphim; from the New Testament Epistles the thrones, dominions, principalities, virtues, and powers; and to these he added angels and archangels to obtain the nine named angelic ranks of being who are the subject of his work the *Celestial Hierarchy*. We need not survey the entire heavenly hierarchy with Denys, but we should take note of the principles of organization underlying his presentation of it. First, in his treatment of the angels closest to God, his emphasis is on God's ineffability. Even the angels nearest God cannot know him

[11] Paul Rorem, *Pseudo-Dionysius: A Commentary on the Texts and an Introduction to Their Influence* (New York: Oxford University Press, 1993). Glenn Peers, *Subtle Bodies: Representing Angels in Byzantium* (Berkeley, Calif.: University of California Press, 2001), considers Pseudo-Dionysius.

completely and hence stand in silence.[12] As the great Cappadocian Fathers and Saint Ephrem the Syrian had taught in the fourth century, knowledge of God is always incomplete and, in eternity, something into which all created being will grow forever.

Denys arranges his nine ranks of angels into three triads, and his second principle of organization is to arrange these triads in turn according to the traditional ascetical schema of purification, illumination, and perfection. He articulates an angelic society ordered to perfection, that is, presents to our view a society of beings something like ourselves but more transparent to God. Early on, ascetics and monks had explained the spiritual life according to this triad: spiritual growth moves from moral purification through illumination to union with God. Probably few would want to defend the details of Denys' schematization, but, as he did for the Church herself in his parallel work, the *Ecclesiastical Hierarchy*, what he has superbly done is to imagine a society actually organized on gospel principles. This of course is a society of angels. The angels are our example of how creatures with free will might rightly order their lives, that is, be holy. But we already know Gregory the Great's claim that we do not simply gaze on the angels from afar, but are united with them in song and worship. Thus it is not too much to say that, though sinners we remain, in a certain sense already now we are bound with the angels in a society striving for perfect understanding, order, and union. Every statement about angels is also a statement about becoming more fully human and Christian.

Above all, the angels teach us the nature of worship. The highest choir, the seraphim, teach us pure worship, for they

---

[12] Andrew Louth, *Denys the Areopagite* (London 1989), 37, cited by Cummings.

are wholly absorbed in God. They show us that though prayer may be about many things, including our own needs, its goal and highest form are the glory of God, worship in which our concerns and ourselves stand back. Such an emphasis on what may be called the vertical dimension of worship, much pursued in both East and West in the early Middle Ages, especially in monasticism, and, once again, caught in Gregory the Great's image of men and angels united in an earth-transcending core or column rising from the altar, the great "Sanctus" or seraphim's song from Isaiah, stands in rather striking contrast to a certain emphasis on a horizontal sense of community commonly found after the Second Vatican Council. This horizontality has rendered our worship mundane, unholy, and egocentric. The early Middle Ages present us an alternative.

The third development that took place in the late Roman and early medieval Church, the growth of the cult of the saints, is closely connected to our topics thus far. Indeed, the saints might be seen as having a common mission with the angels, to return created being, having passed through incarnation and history, to its source in God. Beginning with the period we are examining, the cult of the saints has flourished across the centuries. In the early Middle Ages its growth was luxuriant, and few valleys, territories, diseases, or professions lacked their specific saint, at once a protector and refuge in difficult times and an embodiment of some aspect of God's truth to be emulated. The cult of the saints periodically has changed its focus, sometimes quite properly. Over the last century, for instance, the development of medicine has reduced one of the prime early medieval functions of the saints, help in time of illness. As medicine has shown an increased ability to treat many illnesses, the saints probably have been invoked fewer times as a source of cure. Rather than diminishment of the saints, this might have been viewed as allowing their most central function to stand forth more clearly: embodiment of the many ways in which Christ may be imitated. What happened instead was that, well before Vatican II, certain theologians, sometimes taking the declining petitionary element of the cult for the whole, sometimes for other reasons, worked to reduce the place of the saints in Christian reflection and liturgy. Since the Council, there has been a rejection of the cult without historical precedent. Many Catholics now are no more familiar with the theology of the cult of the saints than they are with the saints themselves.[13] Since my argument is that it is of great importance to revive this cult, to see its function both theologically and at the level of formation of the imagination, I need to say a little about the form the cult took in the late Roman and early medieval world.

The early remembered saints were largely martyrs, but of course the conversion of Emperor Constantine in 312 much reduced the likelihood that holy persons would face literal martyrdom. As the monks were to say in describing their own form of life as a new kind of martyrdom, with Constantine the white martyrdom of a living or lifelong death replaced the red martyrdom of blood. That is, the monk's life, ever spreading from the time of Constantine, was a living martyrdom in which one died to the world, a new form of sanctity. One of the earliest of the nonmartyr (in its literal

---

[13] David Halle, *Inside Culture: Art and Class in the American Home* (Chicago: University of Chicago Press, 1993), 189–91. Colleen McDannell, *Material Christianity Religion and Popular Culture in America* (New Haven, Conn.: Yale University Press, 1995), 173ff., places the attack on the cult of the saints within the larger story of the "simplification" of the liturgy, or stripping of the altars. McDannell, somewhat simplifying herself, takes this to be an attack on feminine characteristics associated with the unreformed Mass.

sense) saints was Saint Martin of Tours, who was born four years after the conversion of Constantine and who died in 397. He is exemplary of the cult of the saints as a record of endless search for ways in which holiness might become incarnate. Martin stands at the head of the history of men trying to respond to and live out missions given by God. He articulates the idea that, to use a later language, every Christian has been given a mission. In the words of the great twentieth-century theologian Hans Urs von Balthasar:[14]

> The Spirit meets the burning questions of the age with an utterance that is the keyword, the answer to the riddle. Never in the form of an abstract statement . . . ; almost always in the form of a new, concrete supernatural mission: the creation of a new saint whose life is a presentation to his own age of the message that heaven is sending to it, a man who is, here and now, the right and relevant interpretation of the Gospel, who is given to this particular age as its way of approach to the perennial truth of Christ. . . . The saints are tradition at its most living, tradition as the word is meant whenever Scripture speaks of the unfolding of the riches of Christ, and the application to history of the norm which is Christ.

History is a stage onto which the saints walk, each with a different God-given part that expresses something of what God is and something of what man may be. They are God's continuing revelation. Each saint's life reveals something universal in something particular. The form that the Christian life takes in this or that saint's life is precipitated by some specific historical moment or human situation. In Martin's case, persecution being at an end, the call was to the

---

[14] *A Theology of History* (San Francisco: Ignatius Press, 1994), 105: see also 72–74, 84–85, 91, 102–5.

conversion of the rural population of Gaul. The cumulative record of the saints' lives is a record of both divine and human inventiveness, of how history has been set to reveal through human actors this or that aspect of what God is. The faith has been delivered once and for all by the apostles, but in a real sense the lives of the saints use the medium of history to continue the revelation of what God is. They make God shine forth in time. Martin illustrates this very well. He shows that, though all Christians are called to sanctity, they are called in unendingly different ways.

After Constantine's cooperation in stopping persecution of Christians and literal martrydom as a means of imitating Christ's life, a new age demanded its own proper forms of sanctity. The imitation of Christ had to take on a shape in Martin's life appropriate to the Constantinian settlement. We might say that the red martyrdom of shedding one's blood in a way that replicated Christ's death on the Cross was replaced with a life of actions conformed to Christ. That is, Martin's life was a living reflection on what form the love of Christ might take in his historical moment. Thus, even with the demise of the cult of the saints today, some know of Martin's Christlike actions, his giving away half of his cloak to a beggar or his kissing of a leper on the lips to give the blessing of God. These both speak to the moment and to the ages. Such actions are in turn imitated by later saints such as Saint Hugh of Lincoln in the twelfth century or Saint Francis of Assisi in the thirteenth, and then become the subject of great works of art. Again and again, Martin's biographer, Sulpicius Severus, emphasized the similarities between Christ and Martin. This is what the cult of the saints is all about: making Christ manifest in one's own age and conforming one's existence to Christ's. This, for Sulpicius, expressed itself not only in Martin's ability to work miracles, but also in his discipline, for instance, his ability to follow an ascetic life while performing the duties of the office of bishop. Sulpicius emphasized that Martin did not allow his administrative duties to get in the way of either his spiritual life or his compassionate ministration to the poor.

Certainly for a modern critical historian there is much that is wrong about many of the saints' lives, much that—even remembering that the primary goal of most saints' lives was not what we would call a factually accurate account—one suspects is factually inaccurate. Sulpicius' life is no exception. The point is not that we should return to some precritical mentality in which we use the saints' lives without criticism, but that, as Jean Leclercq suggested, we meditate not so much on the purported facts of this or that life, but on what image of Christ a given saint was understood to have embodied in his life.[15] The "truth" of a saint's life lies not so much in details as in how he expressed the truth of Christ.

The argument is that we desperately need to know about the saints, about what form others have given to the Christian life. Since time moves on, it is not that we need simply to reiterate the forms of the past, but that we need to form some idea of where we stand in this great cloud of witnesses. Like an Oscar Romero or a Dorothy Day or a Mother Teresa, we will end living a life that could have been lived only in our own day, but like an apprentice artist, we need a well-stocked supply of colors, forms, and subjects if we are to paint paintings. Only if one stands in a living tradition can one form a message that speaks to one's age and across the ages.

---

[15] *The Love of Learning and the Desire for God: A Study of Medieval Monastic Culture*, 3rd ed., trans. Catharine Misrahi (New York: Fordham University Press, 1982), 157–65.

The fourth development, the communion of saints, is closely linked to the third, the cult of the saints. To divest the Church of angels and saints is implicitly an attack also on the idea of the communion of saints, of that body of witnesses both strung out over time, each speaking in a characteristic voice, and, as in Gregory the Great's image, united around the Eucharistic banquet at each moment in time. Since Vatican II, there has been a certain "stripping of the altars" that, on one reading, has tried to center all on Christ. But Christianity is not simply about Christ. It is about the communion of persons, beginning within the Godhead itself. It is about a communion of saints being formed in time with Christ as the head.

If I may be allowed the indulgence of illustrating once more what I have to say by reference to the restored Cathedral of the Madeleine in Salt Lake City, that church has particularly successfully resisted the ravages of liturgical reform during the past generation, the new iconoclasm that has attacked representation of both saint and angel. This church was never whitewashed or pillaged of its decoration in the name of a misconceived Christology, a Christology of the lonely Christ, in which Christ is separated or isolated from his body, the communion of saints. Some time ago I took an out-of-town friend to Mass in this restored Beuern-inspired church, and he exclaimed afterward that the whole history of salvation could be read from the walls alone. Now my friend is a learned man, and I have no illusions about how easy it ever has been for the average person to pick up such a message. Still there was truth in my friend's reaction. In this church, surrounded by angels and saints, the average person cannot but feel himself a member of a vast communion, an actor in a drama still in progress. A certain form of individualism that broods on one's own feelings and reactions, and thinks of these as liturgical "participation", seems in such an environment quite out of place. Indeed, in the presence of such a company, spanning all times and places, Jung-mann's active/passive dichotomy, used to separate the liturgically good from the bad, may not be as fundamental a category as he thought. Such a church perhaps encourages us to think of our fundamental stance as neither active nor passive, but as receptive or contemplative. There is as much difference here as between the beloved who actively receives her lover and the woman who lets him have his way. This—receptivity rather than passiveness as a spiritual stance—of course was the late Roman and early medieval view of wherein lies Christian perfection, especially the perfection of the contemplative monastic life. The soul goes out to God as God comes to the soul.[16] We, especially in the liturgy, are made to receive a gift, to be open to that gift, and all worthy subsequent action is but a response to what we have received. In a society of isolation and individualism, such a church and its liturgy still rise above our horizontal concerns to communicate not only the majesty of God and of God's work, but also the fact that especially here, in this building, God is found, and one enters into a work of the ages.

The idea of the communion of saints worked itself out in all kinds of ways, great and small, in the early Middle Ages. Some may doubt that Gregory the Great's admittedly arresting image of an earth-transcending communion was much more than the high theology of a small elite, the fancy of a Church Father. Rather, in spite of all, in the early Middle Ages what we see is a persistent deepening of understanding of Christianity and the penetration of its so-called high ideas

---

[16] This is very well treated in Leclercq, *Love of Learning*.

into everyday life. Of course much retained the flavor of pre-Christian practice and in the most obvious ways remained resistant to Christianity, but the more one studies the early Middle Ages, the more one is struck by the degree to which in very specific ways over the centuries Christianity really was appropriated outside the relatively sophisticated boundaries that marked monasteries and episcopal residences.

I recently edited a book on the history of marriage during the early Middle Ages, and I want to illustrate this point, the way in which sophisticated theological ideas spread into everyday life, by reference to a development that in that period connected the developing theology of marriage with the doctrine of the communion of saints.[17] The practice, the evolution of the burial practices of married couples, might seem at first glance trivial, but I think it shows very well an attempt to bring Christianity to bear on everyday life. The custom of double sarcophagi, or a tomb in which husband and wife were buried together, was not uncommon among the Romans and was taken over by Christians. Presumably in both cases such usage expressed an idea of marital love. Today if one goes to Les Alyscamps in Arles in southern France, one will see rows of such early Christian double tombs. In Christian usage they express not simply an idea of conjugal love, but the idea that after this life a couple will continue to be together, will continue their communion. Burial practices evolved and varied a great deal during the Middle Ages, and this particular practice of burial of a couple in one sarcophagus largely disappeared. However, the Christianization of death continued.

---

[17] Glenn W. Olsen, ed., *Christian Marriage: A Historical Study* (New York: Herder and Herder, 2001), especially chap. 4.

If we take up the story a couple of centuries later in an area that has been carefully studied, we find the following. In ninth-century Catalonia, the border region that extended from northeastern Spain into southwestern France, couples not only no longer were buried in a common tomb, they were not customarily buried in the same place, even the same city.[18] Heads of aristocratic families or lineages were so important that a deceased man of the aristocracy was commonly buried in the place where his father was buried. That is, in a patrilineal society fathers and sons were buried together. A long-term effect of what has been called the Germanization of life, that is, the introduction into Europe of non-Christian, barbarian understandings of such institutions as marriage, was that, even more than in the Roman world, marriage was part of a family strategy for the acquisition of lands and powerful friends. Women tended to be pawns in this game, and the average aristocrat was bound much more closely to his father than to his wife. The Church, however, century after century preached a different conception, urging that marriage was grounded in a freely given consent of the couple themselves and in conjugal love. Especially from about the middle of the eleventh century, in very specific things such as burial practices, we can see the Church's view spreading. Now husbands and wives begin again to be buried in the same spot, though not in the same tomb. We might say that, relatively speaking, this expressed a weakening of the grip of the father over his children's marriages and a growth of the idea that in marriage the primary communion was between husband and wife.

---

[18] The following summarizes the opening chapters of Martin Aurell, *Les Noces du Comte: Mariage et pouvoir en Catalogne (785–1213)* (Paris: Publications de Sorbonne, 1995).

But Christianity had introduced other closely related ideas of communion that might be thought of as specifications of the general doctrine of the communion of the saints. From the beginning, Christian couples had been told to pray for each other, and this now expressed itself in the idea of a living spouse praying for the salvation of the soul of a departed spouse. It is pretty clear that women were much more faithful in this practice than men. Men tended to remarry after the death of a spouse and with time allowed her memory to fade. Widows tended not to remarry and instead to be the carriers of the memory of the dead. They arranged for prayers for the departed, whether husband or child, and gave alms in their names. That is, women acted as if the former communion in life remained and in the end would overcome death, perhaps even male taciturnity and forgetfulness. Death was in this in some measure Christianized, because it was not only the entrance to eternal life, but also the entrance to perfection of those forms of communion that had begun in this life. Certainly none of this expressed grand theological ideas in any fullness, but all of it showed a continuing reflection on Christianity that led to understanding more areas of life in a Christian way. We who lament the de-Christianization of life today but do not even think to place some icon or image of one of the saints on our living room wall for our children to gaze on might reflect on these little, everyday ways in which earlier life was Christianized.

The fifth and final development is the shape the liturgy took in the early Middle Ages. According to Jungmann, over the course of the Middle Ages the liturgy drifted from the active participation of the patristic period to an inert and unalert passivity that characterized both layman and priest by the end of the Middle Ages. This process, the argument runs, was well advanced by the close of the period of interest here, the early Middle Ages. Had I sufficient space, I would quarrel a bit with Jungmann's characterization and note the degree to which the views of this Austrian Jesuit embody traditional Protestant perspectives on the Middle Ages and on what a desirable Christianity should look like. Lacking this, I will follow a more limited but very perceptive analysis made of Jungmann by Eamon Duffy, who, while recognizing the greatness of Jungmann's scholarship, nevertheless believes that this analysis seems to [19]

> fall down disastrously . . . in his assumption that in this whole process the laity and their local clergy were passive and inert, progressively excluded from an understanding of the "true" meaning of the sacraments and from participation in the "right" sort of liturgical celebration, at the mercy of the reduced and impoverished sacramental and liturgical catechesis offered by the medieval church, so that they became, in Jungmann's phrase, "not much more than spectators".

According to Duffy, this represents a serious misunderstanding of what liturgy is for and how it operates and has had all kinds of unfortunate effects both on the treatment of liturgy at the Second Vatican Council itself and on post-Vatican II liturgical reform. In Jungmann's point of view, which has been tremendously influential, there is an underlying assumption that liturgy is essentially didactic, a means of instructing the faithful and bringing them into intelligent, active participation in the worship of the Church. Such a view is not so much simply wrong—who does not want a well-instructed laity and clergy?—as constricted in its view of what liturgy is

---

[19] Roberts, "The Stripping of the Altars and the Liturgy", 2–3 (see above, no. 1), describing a lecture by Duffy. The following quotations are all from Roberts' summary, typographically corrected.

and how it achieves its ends, especially in an oral culture such as, outside the restricted circles of clergy and monk, we largely find in the early Middle Ages.

This last point needs elaboration. Oronzo Giordano has suggested, in one sense turning Jungmann's views on their head, that what we find in the Carolingian period, that is, in the late eighth and ninth centuries, is a liturgical civilization.[20] Especially Charlemagne had attempted to legislate a Christian form for life, for instance, insisting on the obligation to keep Sunday holy. He issued long lists of activities that were prohibited or suspended that all might preserve the honor and rest of the Lord's day. Thus in certain respects Carolingian civilization was liturgical, for, as in the case of the keeping of the Lord's Day, no matter how many, as the records also tell us, stayed away from church or came to church only to chat, or were "passive" before a drama in which the priest was the chief actor, everyday life, starting with its sense of time, was shaped by Christian liturgy. Whatever the persistence of folklore and of variation in how the liturgy itself was said, a "Christian people" collectively practiced generically the same rites. As Étienne Delaruelle has said, in a society in which few were literate the liturgy was effectively law, exegesis, history, and theology—and, one might add, increasingly drama, gesture, and color.

Liturgical reformers in the twentieth century such as Jungmann have not always been happy about especially what they take to have been the passivity of the laity in the early Middle Ages, but much of their criticism is historically unsophisticated. First, Augustine and many of the Church

<hr />

[20] Oronzo Giordano, *Religiosidad popular en la Edad Media*, trans. Pilar García Mouton and Valentín García Yebra (Madrid: Gredos, 1983), 36–37, 48 on the following.

Fathers had complained repeatedly about the inattention of their congregations, so we should not idealize the patristic situation. This was before or just at the beginning of the inundation of Europe by the barbarian peoples. The average Carolingian was the child of these latter peoples and came from a culture that lacked or never had had interiority or a certain discipline needed for some forms of active participation.[21] Thinking was according to a kind of group mentality. Any other attitudes would have to be learned over an extended period of time. One defined oneself not so much as an individual but as a member of larger entities: families and peoples. Likely the family of an eighth- or ninth-century person had been pagan in the recent past. For such a person, whose whole culture was foreign to the individualistic categories beloved of twentieth-century liturgical reformers, to see good liturgy as active and bad as passive misses the point. The individual Carolingian resonated with his group and experienced the liturgy in a group. Without more evidence than we have, it is no better to call this orientation passive than active. Stress on the communion of saints, on the saints and angels who surrounded him, was precisely a way in which such a person could find in Christianity something that made sense, could see Christianity as family and people.

The kind of ahistorical demands Jungmann made of early medieval people embodied, according to Duffy,

---

[21] I have noted exceptions in "Christian Perfection and *transitus ad monasterium* in Lupus of Ferrières' *Letter 29*", in *Proceedings of the Eighth International Congress of Medieval Canon Law*, University of California, San Diego, Aug. 20–27, 1988 (*Monumenta iuris canonici, series C: Subsidia*, vol. 9, Vatican City: Bibloteca Apostolica Vaticana, 1991), 355–68, and in "One Heart and One Soul (Acts 4:32 and 34) in Dhuoda's *Manual*", *Church History* 61 (1992): 23–33.

an understanding of liturgy as a form of painless catechesis, a forum for teaching, with a consequent subordination of its doxological character to its teaching value. Some such notion ... I think, lies behind the [Second Vatican] Council's stipulation that, for educational reasons, a "noble simplicity" was to be the keynote of all liturgical reform. It has certainly underlain much of the relentless didacticism which characterizes so many modern celebrations of the liturgy, in which we are *directed* to the meanings which we are to take away whether from the rite or the readings.

Duffy's argument is that

in fact liturgy rarely works by simplicity, as such. It works by symbolic word and gesture, and it is of the essence of a symbol, as opposed say to an allegory, that it is polyphonic, polysemic.

In addition, rituals and liturgies are

by their very nature traditional. . . . Liturgies, therefore, are palimpsests which grow by accretion, by the overlaying and juxtaposition of layer upon layer of meaning and sign, which are often in tension with each other, and held together not by a single dominant explanation but by performance . . . through which we appropriate and enter into the web of realities symbolized within the rite, by which we live within the tradition. . . . To attempt to eliminate from our liturgies what we do not understand or cannot presently appropriate is always fraught with danger, for it runs the risk of reducing the polyphony of the rite to a thin monotone.

If we succumb to such perspectives, Duffy holds, we are likely to envision tradition "as a prison-house rather than a power-house":

Too much attention was paid [by Jungmann and people who thought similarly] to text and rubric in liturgical rites, too little to the concrete embedding of liturgy in social reality, and the complex uses to which the Christian people actually put the language of liturgy and sacrament. In the process, liturgical theorists gave too little value to the paraliturgical proliferation of secondary rites, and what they thought of as the clutter of sacramentals which ... was a sign not of decadence but of vigorous lay appropriation of the meaning of the liturgy.... For the laity, with an instinct which ... was by no means naive or misguided, often fixed on those very elements within the liturgy which the liturgists judged to be marginal, and which modern reforms have planed away as accretions and corruptions, in the name of "noble simplicity" and a fundamentalist and too narrow understanding of the return to sources.

In sum, to speak in my own voice, it seems to me that we could learn a great deal from late Roman and early medieval culture about how liturgy is to function in life. Jungmann deplored how, starting in the early Middle Ages, the liturgy was constantly elaborated so that its patristic simplicity was lost and it became a kind of dense forest of allegory in which one could easily lose one's way. That is, it no longer bore a clear message, but became a kind of polyphony or even cacophany of many messages. Jungmann's description here was accurate enough, though—ironically—he insufficiently recognized how catechetical the intent was of the Carolingian reformers.[22] However, his evaluation of what happened must be disputed. He spoke of the laity and local clergy as passive and saw what he called "liturgical allegorization" as the work of a small elite.[23] It seems to me that this is exactly what we

---

[22] Halle, *Inside Culture*, as at 7, shows for a very different subject matter that cultural products in general do not have only one basic set of meanings.

[23] Josef A. Jungmann, *The Mass of the Roman Rite: Its Origins and Development*, trans. Francis A. Brunner, 2 vols. (New York: Christian Classics, 1951),

would expect at a point in history when a largely oral culture was learning a new religion at the hand of a small literate class. That especially monks were highly inventive in elaborating the liturgy following the same patterns they used in scriptural exegesis, in which we find layer after layer of interpretation of a single text, spiritual sense following on literal, is not at all surprising. This is not the sign of an increasing isolation or passivity of the laity, who in these matters, if we are speaking of Celtic and Germanic peoples, had never been "active", but of the rich spiritual life of those forming them. Jean Leclercq once observed that the development of Christian doctrine historically has been driven less by scholastic or academic reflection than by loving and praying hearts, especially monastic hearts, driven to plumb all the beauty of revelation.[24] So my first comment is that what Jungmann laments as a loss of liturgical simplicity is better seen as the record of many ardent hearts trying to grasp the faith more and more and, where circumstance allowed, spread it to laymen previously outside its ambit.

Much better than many modern liturgists, the early medieval liturgist understood that the liturgy is not at base a form of catechesis at all, but an instrument of worship. Early medieval people had no trouble living with what we call polyvalent or polysemic texts. That is, because it was—one is tempted to say, instinctively—understood that the primary function of liturgy is to worship, not to instruct, texts could bear many simultaneous meanings. They did not have to be

I, 87. For recent scholarship on the educational goals of Carolingian liturgical reform, see Rosamond McKitterick, *The Frankish Church and the Carolingian Reforms, 789–895* (London: Royal Historical Society, 1977), as at 129–47, and Susan A. Keefe, *Water and the Word: Baptism and the Education of the Clergy in the Carolingian Empire* (Notre Dame, Ind.: University of Notre Dame Press, 2002).

[24] *Love of Learning*, 209ff.

simple or univocal. Liturgy was understood to be more like wisdom literature than like a manual of instruction or of theology. Just as wisdom literature mulls over all that can be said about a subject, even if contradictory, liturgy rarely has one simple message. It is rather a body of accumulated prayer, practice, and meditation, in which any one message is constantly complicated by new thoughts, by drawing new connections between the things that are expressed in it. It is more witness to the majesty of God than to his comprehensibility. I would not deny that—as by the time of Trent—the liturgy might become such a dense undergrowth that some pruning might be in order, but early medieval people could hardly see this. My argument is that, throughout the Middle Ages, its growth is witness to spiritual vitality and that in some ways, in a period in which much was not written, it is our record of popular as well as monastic devotion. For we should remember that the liturgy is not simply the Mass, but includes all those hymns and devotions, all those sacramentals, perhaps said at a saint's shrine, that reach down through society to touch unlearned and learned alike. What has sometimes been said of the paintings that decorated medieval church walls is much truer of the liturgy, that it is the poor or illiterate man's Bible. In the early Middle Ages, at a time when few could read or afford a Bible, the liturgy was the Word, that is, the means by which Christ was communicated in tangible fashion. The difficulty modern scholars have had in understanding exactly the place of the liturgy in that society should caution us against merely didactic prescriptions for its place in ours.

III

High Medieval Christianity:
An Assessment from the Beginning
of the Third Millennium

Millennial dates are only symbolic, and in any case if the scholars are right, the third millennium of the Christian era began several years before our calendar indicates. When in the sixth century the monk and canonist Dionysius Exiguus brought the Alexandrian nineteen-year Easter cycle to Rome and the West and replaced the era of Diocletian with that of Christ, he apparently miscalculated Christ's birth by four to seven years.[1] Thus an irony of the dating system that made Christ's birth central to human history and the point from which everything was to be measured is that Dionysius got it wrong. Christ was in fact born sometime between seven and four years "before Christ". At the latest, the "second millennium" ended in 1996. But of course we know that scholars are always ruining the party and that in any case millennial dates are simply occasions for measuring things, taking inventories, and making guesses about or expressing our hopes for the future. Our predecessors tried

---

[1] V. Loi, "Dionysius Exiguus," *Encyclopedia of the Early Church*, ed. Angelo Di Berardino, trans. Adrian Walford, with a foreword and bibliographic amendments by W. H. C. Frend, 2 vols. (New York: Oxford University Press, 1992), I, 237.

to estimate the significance of the year 1000, and we recently tried to measure the significance of 2000.

What I would like to do in the present chapter is take stock of the high Middle Ages defined as a period beginning with the so-called Gregorian reform of the later eleventh century and ending with the Jubilee year of 1300, an earlier symbolic date proclaimed by Pope Boniface VIII. I wish from the vantage point of the early third millennium to reflect on the significance of the deeds of our medieval predecessors. Since we see in a glass darkly, the goal is not to form some ultimate and definitive judgment on the historical record, but to reflect on that mysterious tapestry of history in which God has been through time intertwining light thread with dark. Because of the mixed quality of all historical achievement, my goal is as much humiliating or sobering as anything else. Clearly there are no unalloyed victories or definitive successes in time. What seems success by one standard of measurement seems failure by another. Indeed, in history each success seems to include the seeds of its future failure or demise.

Some medieval people could see this. At Saint Bonaventure's election as general of the Franciscan order in the midthirteenth century, he wrote in a letter to the minister provincial that though in some respects the order had progressed, in others it had declined. Bonaventure thought he saw in this a pattern in which over time all religious orders tend to lose their first state of perfection. In reply the minister provincial offered an elaborate reflection on a kind of law of history, that a new order, beginning in great enthusiasm and commitment, would within a couple of generations experience decline.[2] Each

[2] The classic exposition is Etienne Gilson, *The Philosophy of St. Bonaventure*, trans. Illtyd Trethowan and Frank J. Sheed (Paterson, N.J.: St. Anthony Guild Press, 1965), 56–57.

human achievement has its dark side, its undesirable effects, and its limitations. Balance and equipoise seem forever to elude us. We ourselves are in history and have no way of arising above it to some fixed and stable perch from which we could pass final judgment on earlier men. In this spirit the Methodist historian Herbert Butterfield thought the divine command "judge not that ye be not judged" addressed directly to historians.[3] Things look one way when seen from within the first flush of their coming to be, quite another way after a century has passed, and different again from the viewpoint of a millennium.

The high Middle Ages achieved so much that the present essay must be very selective in what it considers. It centers on three interrelated developments, each of them in fact quite vast: (1) the increasing exploration of the doctrine of the Incarnation, especially as revealed in the formulation of distinctly Christian political and economic principles; (2) the development of Scholasticism; and (3) the growth of subjectivity in religion. To turn to the first development, two generations ago the great German Lutheran historian Gerd Tellenbach suggested that the single most significant turning point in the history of Christianity occurred during our period, namely, the investiture struggle of the later eleventh century.[4] Tellenbach's argument was that, when all is said and done, until the time of Gregory VII (1073–1085), Christianity either had followed the world-fleeing impulse embodied in the monastic life or, in one possible understanding of the commandment to "render unto Caesar the things that are Caesar's", had acquiesced in leaving the world's governance

---

[3] *Christianity and History* (New York: Scribner, 1950), 63–91.

[4] *Church, State and Christian Society at the Time of the Investiture Contest*, trans. R. F. Bennett (Oxford: Blackwell, 1959).

to God-chosen lay kings and emperors.[5] In the former case, Christianity's task had not been seen as incarnational or world transforming. In the latter case of conversion of the world by a divinely instituted monarch, a certain incarnationalism had been present, but one in which the Church was led rather than leader.

Charlemagne (768–814) had thought it part of his duties as God chosen to instruct the Pope in the government of the Church. Then, Tellenbach argued, with Gregory VII Popes and priests began to dream of a right ordering of the world in which monarchs would relinquish government of the Church to restrict themselves to the lay tasks for which they were specifically qualified. The ecclesiastical hierarchy as bearers of the sacraments and interpreters of the Gospel would bear prime responsibility for giving society a Christian form. From being primarily a religion that was either world withdrawing or acquiesced in lay control of its internal life, Christianity became under its priests and Popes a world-reordering religion.

Tellenbach's suggestion was very audacious, and the more one thinks about it, the more one finds it needs qualifications of various kinds.[6] Yet there does seem something right in the observation, developed by Gerhart Ladner, that an-

[5] John A. F. Thomson, *The Western Church in the Middle Ages* (New York: Oxford University Press, 1998), 32–99, gives an up-to-date picture of the difficulties faced by the tenth- and eleventh-century Church in regard to lay control, and of the Gregorian reform.

[6] See especially Colin Morris, *The Papal Monarchy: The Western Church from 1050 to 1250* (Oxford: Oxford University Press, 1989), index under "Gregorian reform, concept of", with my review in *The Catholic Historical Review* 77 (1991): 503–5, and John Howe, *Church Reform and Social Change in Eleventh-Century Italy: Dominic of Sora and His Patrons* (Philadelphia: University of Pennsylvania Press, 1997), xv–xvi, a good statement of the limitations of Tellenbach's views.

cient Christianity tended to conceive of reform in terms of the transformation or reform of individuals; while without abandoning this earlier interest the Gregorian reform of the eleventh century especially concerned itself with the reform of society itself, but under the leadership of the Church rather than of monarchs.[7] Certainly earlier rulers such as Constantine (312–337), Charlemagne, or the tenth-century Ottonians had expressed a kind of incarnational impulse, in which they wished their peoples imbued with Christian teaching. The Gregorian papacy went far beyond this.

By Gregory's time, Western Europe had largely been at least superficially Christianized, and most people thought of themselves as Christians.[8] A language of *Christianitas* or Christendom had been developing since Carolingian times, but now Gregory posed to Christian Europeans a kind of structural or ordering question, "How should Christianity form our life together?" This question expressed a new intensity of incarnational impulse, which was to be replicated in many areas of life, for instance, in the tendency from the thirteenth century of new religious orders to turn to or minister within the world rather than flee it. The Franciscans and Dominicans in the thirteenth century abandoned the vow of stability, the vow earlier monks had taken to live their lives withdrawn from society and within a cloister, and became more world entering, active, and urban than earlier monks. In the sixteenth century the Jesuits would go even further

---

[7] *The Idea of Reform: Its Impact on Christian Thought in the Age of the Fathers*, rev. ed. (New York: Harper and Row, 1967).

[8] For a comparison of older and newer approaches to the Christianization and formation of Europe, see my "The Changing Understanding of the Making of Europe from Christopher Dawson to Robert Bartlett," published in one form in *Quidditas* 20 (1999): 159–70, and in another in *Actas del V Congreso "Cultura Europea"* (Pamplona, Spain: Thomson Aranzadi, 2000), 203–10.

and be more concerned with "finding God in all things" than had been any of the thirteenth-century orders.

One could go so far as to say that the genius or defining characteristic of Christianity in the second millennium was its mission to transform the world, to evangelize the world as well as individuals. Earlier centuries had tended to see Christianity as one more—albeit a very important—ingredient introduced into the body politic as it formed historically. It gave new life and vigor, but to the end of preserving such old ideals as *Romanitas*, the Roman way of life and system of values. Though recent scholarship has shown that in the late Roman and early medieval world emperors such as Constantine and bishops such as Caesarius of Arles (470?–542) gave thought to such things as giving the cities they lived in a Christian topography shaped around Christian buildings, imagination had not normally extended to the idea that life in all its social and political dimensions could be reordered by the Gospel.[9] Similarly, in the Middle Ages, while bishops continued to give thought to the way in which buildings might "speak for God" and articulate a Christian presence and claims to authority, they far from commonly concluded to radical rejection of inherited social norms.[10]

[9] On Constantine see Charles Odahl, "God and Constantine: Divine Sanction for Imperial Rule in the First Christian Emperor's Early Letters and Art", *The Catholic Historical Review* 81 (1995): 327–52, and John Curran, *Pagan City and Christian Capital: Rome in the Fourth Century* (New York: Oxford University Press, 2002); and on Caesarius, William E. Klingshirn, *Caesarius of Arles: The Making of a Christian Community in Late Antique Gaul* (New York: Cambridge University Press, 1994). J. H. W. G. Liebeschuetz, *Decline and Fall of the Roman City* (New York: Oxford University Press, 2001), is a Gibbonesque book, written from the perspective of loss of the classical: see the rejoinder by Raymond Van Dam in a review in *Church History* 71 (2002): 873–75.

[10] Maureen C. Miller, *The Bishop's Palace: Architecture and Authority in Medieval Italy* (Ithaca, N.Y.: Cornell University Press, 2000). See also John Howe,

Certainly in founding their "cities in the desert" some of the monks had from the first asked what a life built wholly on Gospel principles would look like, but their answers tended to express themselves in categories that despaired of the world rather than expressed confidence in its possible Christian re-shaping. Similarly, throughout the first Christian millennium many saints opposed received values, envisioning, especially as they neared 1000, for instance, the Christian life as peace making rather than war making.[11] Still, the tendency was to think more in categories of individual than of social reform. Charlemagne could add to the liturgical Christianization of time that had already taken place legislation in favor of keeping Sunday holy, but heartily resisted any notion that his own position vis-à-vis priests and Popes might need rethinking. There was a strong disposition in favor of "good old custom".

Then the Gregorian reformers of the eleventh century asked whether, in the light of Christianity, what had been received from the past stood in need of radical restructuring, even uprooting. Their cry was "Christ said, 'I am the Truth.' He did not say, 'I am the custom', but 'I am the Truth.'"[12] Their notion of reform was as much structural as personal. If—as all things human—the tendency to wish the world

---

"Creating Symbolic Landscapes: Medieval Development of Sacred Space", in *Inventing Medieval Landscapes: Sense of Place in Western Europe* (Gainesville, Fla.: University of Florida, 2002), 208–23.

[11] *The Peace of God: Social Violence and Religious Response in France Around the Year 1000*, ed. Thomas Head and Richard Landes (Ithaca, N.Y.: Cornell University Press, 1992).

[12] For variations of this battle cry, found throughout the eleventh and twelfth centuries, see my "John of Salisbury's Humanism", in *Gli Umanesimi Medievali*, ed. Claudio Leonardi (Florence: SISMEL Edizioni del Galluzzo, 1998), 447–68 at 463–65.

remade in the image of Christ had unexpected and un-
desired results and was in the second millennium to express
itself in dark as well as glorious things, and if in some significant ways the evangelical impulse faltered in the second
half of the twentieth century, at the turn to the third millennium the Church continued to have a Pope who presented Christianity as a world-transforming religion. Thus
Tellenbach's claim that to the present there has never been as
significant a redirection of Christian impulse as found in the
Gregorian reform.

The investiture struggle, which Tellenbach saw as at base
a struggle over *libertas ecclesiae*, freedom of the Church, was a
defining series of events that separated the early from the
high Middle Ages. One writer has gone so far as to say, "The
great Catholic battle of the modern era has been for *libertas
ecclesiae*—the liberty of the Church to govern itself." [13] Because this struggle centered on the question of what a society ordered by the Gospel would look like, study of it is in
part study of the question of what Christianity desires of the
political order. This raises in turn the question of whether
the high Middle Ages permanently achieved, at least as a
clarification of thought, some great truth about political life.
Only an integralist, someone who believes we can really re-

---

[13] Richard John Neuhaus, "The Persistence of the Catholic Moment", *First
Things*, no. 130 (Feb. 2003): 26–30 at 26. In this article Neuhaus reasserts the
arguments made in his earlier *The Catholic Moment: The Paradox of the Church in
the Postmodern World* (San Francisco: Harper and Row, 1987), reviewed by me
in "The Catholic Moment?" (*Communio: International Catholic Review* 15 [1988]:
474–87), while stating such things as that "Catholicism [today] in the public
square is weakened by its gradual *but certain* [italics mine] sociological accommodation to a Protestant ethos ... that construes religion in terms of con-
sumer preference and voluntary associations in support of those preferences"
(26). Apparently his book should have been named *The Protestant Moment*.

cover the life of some earlier age in an established Church, could think that, if it had, we could return to it. That is not our goal. Rather, the investiture struggle raises the question of whether eleventh-century people discovered principles applicable to any political order in which Christians live or principles by which the flaws of any order can be discovered.

The immediate question in the eleventh century was whether the Church had the right to select her own bishops or whether Henry IV of Germany and the other monarchs of Europe could continue in longstanding theocratic fashion to do this. Monarchy, as we have noted, had always been sacral. The traditional claim from the side of Christian monarchs had been that because Christian kings rule by the grace and in the name of God, they are responsible for godly order in all areas of life, including that of the Church. The Christian monarch is a minister of God who supervises even the sacramental and priestly order, and on the last day he must account to God for all.

Against such a view, Gregory presented another logic.[14] This too had long historical roots and arguably was a new form of the question of Matthew's Gospel, "What must I do to be perfect?" The original question, that asked of Christ by the rich young man, had wanted to know what form an unreserved discipleship would take. What would a life look like that was unreservedly built on the gospel, as opposed to the inherited institutions of man? Monasticism had been the most common historical reply to this question. Gregory took the question to a new level by asking what the implications

---

[14] All Gregory's letters have been translated by H. E. J. Cowdrey: *The Register of Pope Gregory VII 1073–1085: An English Translation* (New York: Oxford University Press, 2002). See also Cowdrey's *Pope Gregory VII, 1073–85* (New York: Oxford University Press, 1998).

of the gospel were, not for an individual life, but for society itself.

What it would not look like was the theocratic monarchy of traditional Germanic society. If the goal of human life is to have as many enter the Kingdom of God as possible, and the Kingdom is entered through the sacramental system, then obviously, Gregory concluded, the work of priests is higher than that of kings. Rather than the Church being controlled by the state, as she was in theocratic monarchy, the Church must be free by her best lights to lead all to the Kingdom. At the least the Church has to be independent of the state. She must be free to choose her own leaders, hence the struggle over investiture of bishops. In this view, it was the Church that represented the higher principle, and though Gregory had no desire to replace royal government of the world with papal government of the world, he did wish that monarchs modify their traditional claims to supervise the Church and acknowledge that they were mere men ruling for lay, temporal, or innerworldly ends.

Unfortunately a strain of Catholic thought some call neoconservative and some, more appropriately, neoliberal persistently continues to the present to misinform people about these issues, speaking as if the papal goal from the eleventh century was temporal world rulership, the replacement of lay with papal theocracy, rather than the assertion of the intrinsic superiority of the ecclesiastical to the political principle.[15] Western history here is reduced to a struggle between

---

[15] Richard John Neuhaus, " 'We Hold These Truths'—An Argument to Be Engaged", *First Things*, no. 77 (Nov. 1997): 66–73 at 70. Alongside all the other errors Neuhaus makes in two paragraphs of description, his lack of awareness of the prolonged debate, going back more than half a century, over the authorship and intention of the *Dictatus papae* seems almost minor. For en-

"monism" and "pluralism" and Gregory taken to be an example of a monism of Christendom at its peak.[16] On the contrary, the Christian king was for Gregory and generally for the Gregorian party normally to rule by his own best lights. No Chestertonian papal bulls were to be expected at the breakfast table, for the papacy had no special competence in things temporal. But, according to Gregory, all Christian rulers were under God and were, as Christians, to be held to the moral law and the teachings of the Church. In matters of grave violation of justice or Church teaching, the ecclesiastical hierarchy could call kings to account, judge them unworthy of office, and work for their deposition. That is, in conflicts between the lower goods aimed at by the state and the higher goods aimed at by the priesthood and the sacramental system, though the Church had no customary right to rule temporally, she did have a right to intervene in secular matters in the cause of justice and for the salvation of souls.

Gregory's views raise at least two questions: (1) whether his logic was a true logic always valid, if perhaps needing further development and contextual specification, and (2) whether the unforeseen, perhaps unwanted, subsequent growing desacralization of European life that some have seen as

trance to this debate, and the theory that the *Dictatus* is the index to a now lost canonical collection, see Stephan Kuttner, "Liber canonicus", *Studi Gregoriani* 2 (1947): 387–401.

[16] There are further bibliography and discussion in the entry "Gregory VII, Pope (1073–85)", by Uta-Renate Blumenthal and in my "Introduction" and "Bibliographic Note", to "Part II: The Medieval Papacy", in *The Great Popes through History: An Encyclopedia*, ed. Frank Coppa, 2 vols. (Westport, Conn., 2002), vol. 1, 73–177. See on Neuhaus' usage of monism, Olsen, "The Catholic Moment?" 474–87, and further my "The 'Catholic Moment' and the Question of Inculturation", in *Catholicity and the New Evangelization* (Steubenville, Ohio: Fellowship of Catholic Scholars, 1995), 17–54.

implicit in Gregory's insistence that kings were merely laymen should have been expected. We turn to these questions
in reverse order. The traditional Germanic view that the king
represents God held that he was to be obeyed come what
may. In a Christian form, this view proposed that "obeying
the powers that be" was a straightforward question of doing
what the king said, even if one had reservations about its
goodness. Gregory agreed that the king "ruled by grace",
but denied that this meant that the king had always to be
obeyed. Gregory lived too early to possess a fully articulated
natural law doctrine of a scholastic form, but he held that
since the royal office existed to promote rather than under-
mine the will of God, a king who significantly departed from
either justice (the natural goals of government) or the teaching of the Church (the supernatural goods God wishes for
all men) was not to be obeyed. Kingship was not sacral if
that meant that whatever the king did was by that fact God
authorized and to be obeyed. The king was a mere man and
was to be held to the same moral and rational standards as
other men. Since he also claimed to be a Christian, he was
to abide by the teachings of the Church as much as any other
Christian.

Though when Gregory took on Henry of Germany in
the name of freedom of the Church no one could have seen
the long-term implications of this, a number of writers have
described Gregory's position as desacralizing the royal office,
and thence political life more generally. Although they have
not all meant quite the same thing, it seems clear to me that
Gregory's position did do this. When Gregory, wishing the
Church to be free to select her own bishops, declared the
king of Germany to be a mere man and his empire an institution founded in fratricide, in sin (the allusion is both to
Virgil and Augustine, to Romulus and Remus, and to Cain

and Abel), this was to the end of denying to the king a divine sanction that had always to be obeyed. Gregory thus contributed to a larger process of desacralization of the political order that is still working its way out today. But his intention was more specific than this, not to separate Church from state, but more clearly to distinguish what is proper to each, their specific jurisdictions.

As stated, some writers have seen in Gregory's position the secularization of politics generally or have argued that in the long run Christianity—or perhaps just some form of it, as Protestantism—inevitably moves toward secularization. This raises more issues than can be addressed here, some of which will be considered again in Chapter Five. The short response is that, yes, Gregory did secularize the royal office and make it essentially an office of this world. Yet, though this was one factor in later European secularization, it was minor in comparison to, say, the Wars of Religion of the seventeenth century. In its own terms Gregory achieved what might be called a proper secularization, because he showed that politics of its nature is a thing of the *saeculum*, of the passing age, and simply not as important as the order of salvation. This may be clarified by taking up the other question about Gregory to which we have already alluded, whether his argument for a right order in which in some sense the Church is superior to the state has some permanent validity.

All through the Middle Ages there was a tendency to equate the Church with her hierarchy.[17] This "clericalism" has persisted in Catholicism to the present, though Vatican II

---

[17] See Yves M. J. Congar, *L'ecclésiologie du haut Moyen-Age: De Saint Grégoire le Grand à la désunion entre Byzance et Rome* (Paris, 1968), and *Lay People in the Church: A Study for a Theology of Laity*, trans. Donald Attwater, 2nd ed. (Westminster, Md.: Newman Press, 1967).

struggled mightily to unseat it in favor of the idea that the Church is the whole people of God. Granted Gregory VII's instinctive tendency to identify the Church with her hierarchy, and admitting the need for a more ample view here in the spirit of Vatican II, I see nothing wrong with the essential lines of Gregory's argument for freedom of the Church. To reduce it to its essentials, all men are made for eternal life, and the entrance to eternal life is through the sacraments, first of all baptism, but then through the whole sacramental system over which the priesthood presides. Since the goal of the sacramental system, eternal life, is intrinsically superior to all goals of temporal government, peace, justice, and the like, at the least the *sacerdotium* must be independent of the *regnum*. But since the Church pursues intrinsically higher goals, in some sense she is superior to the state, is the state's judge in the matters already specified. I understand subsequent medieval Church-state theory and conflict to be a working out of what this sense of a proper superiority might be. There was of course a variety of opinion, but there also was a principal view, already evident in Gregory's writings. This itself pointed to a proper secularization, for it allowed a relative autonomy to the lower principle, the state.

To be brief, the view to which Gregory and subsequent Popes most commonly inclined was that the goals of Church and state were both legitimate and sufficiently different to justify a permanent division of labor. Scholars of the Middle Ages have not agreed on a label to be put on this view, but probably most commonly have called it *dualism*.[18] To think

---

[18] There is a useful discussion in Brian Tierney, *The Crisis of Church and State 1050–1300* (Englewood Cliffs, N.J.: Prentice Hall, 1964), 1–5, and see Gaines Post, *Studies in Medieval Legal Thought: Public Law and the State, 1100–1322* (Princeton, N.J.: Princeton University Press, 1964), esp. chap. 11. There

of Gregory as what Richard John Neuhaus calls a "monist" seriously obfuscates the issues and Gregory's position. That is, the eventual elucidation of the question of the desired relation between Church and state sometimes associated with Thomas Aquinas (1225–1274), but more properly and fully with Leo XIII (1810–1903), was a refinement of views long held and long developing. Certain natural goods such as peace, justice, education, and more generally the common good are sufficiently comprehensible by unaided human reason that they can be pursued by a government of this world. The Church, specifically the priesthood, has no particular competence in such matters and thus should resist all temptation to usurp a proper secularization in which laymen look after worldly affairs. But because laymen, kings, might do grave evil or work against human salvation, the Church has the right in matters of sufficient gravity, when gross injustice is threatened or salvation imperiled, to intervene in the temporal order.

In such a theory, Church is not separated from state, but distinguished from it or harmonized with it. The natural or political order has only a proper or limited autonomy, not a simple independence. As in the earlier theory developed by Pope Gelasius I (492–96) and still affirmed in the Byzantine world in the eleventh century, normally, the two orders, each pursuing its proper competence or area of primary

---

clearly is a terminological problem here. To use "dualism" in the sense I am using it is common among students of the Middle Ages, but for the student of American history "dualism" may evoke visions of something quite different, the disestablishment of religion and separation of powers. Rather than abandoning the term, I would ask the reader to remember that I am using it to designate the differentiation—not separation—between temporal and spiritual jurisdictions that most post-Gregorian medieval ecclesiastical writers championed.

jurisdiction—*spiritualia* on the one hand, *temporalia* on the other—are to aid the other in the other's area of primary jurisdiction. Again, the theory is harmony, not separation, of Church and state. The goal is not the compartmentalization of life, but the integration of its various spheres. Men are seen as living in one Christian society, which has two kinds of authority within it.

How does such a theory look from the beginning of the third millennium? Some, probably most, would say that it is passé. I do not think this is so and see both of Gregory's basic distinctions with their later papal and canonical refinements as a precious and enduring achievement, which should always make us uncomfortable about any claim that in American history we have found a better way. We may have done what we had to do to live together, but that is quite a different question. That is, it seems to me a kind of provincialism to see in the disestablishment found in the American tradition a more perfect form of the specification of how grace is to relate to nature than in the ongoing story of "dualism".[19] But Catholicism in America has been so coopted by the "American experiment" that almost the whole spectrum of American Catholic interpretation declares, for instance, that *Dignitatis Humanae*, 22, that is, the "Declaration

---

[19] What I mean by this is that, though clearly in certain parts of the world, above all Europe, there has been a secularizing tendency in which the idea of a division of labor between Church and state is for some laughable because all claims of the Church are largely rejected; in many countries down to the present (Canada and Germany would be examples), and in the papal encyclical tradition, there have been more generous constructions of the desired relation between church and state, which tend to view both parties as within a single society and thus more to be harmonized than separated in the American liberal sense. The ideal is division of labor and cooperation more than a "high wall of separation": see further my "Separating Church and State", *Faith and Reason* 20 (1994): 403–25.

on Religious Freedom" of Vatican II, rules out the confessional state.[20] Thus liberalism rewrites and denies the explicit teaching of the encyclical tradition of the nineteenth and twentieth centuries, making Vatican II mark a decisive break with that tradition and acceptance of the liberal ideal of a state ordered—if that is the right word—around the ideal of individual liberties. Again, history may have ruled out confessional states in our part of the world, but that is quite a different matter. To think that other societies are somehow deficient because they have more communal values, less emphasis on liberty, or a larger agreement about religion than do we arguably is just one more expression of that combination of arrogance and ignorance that many find so insufferable in Americans. It also likely expresses a certain irrealism about the world, an attitude which, instead of appreciating the profoundly different ways in which various societies have developed, wishes them all to copy "the city set on a hill".

One of the great labors of the post-Gregorian history of dualism, standing now most clearly revealed in the thought of John Paul II, has been the working out of the place of religious freedom in proper evangelization. I wish I had the space here to show that this is inadequately described as a new route taken in the modern period; it is as much a project

---

[20] I have pursued these unseasonable thoughts in such essays as "The Meaning of Christian Culture: A Historical View", in *Catholicism and Secularization in America: Essays on Nature, Grace, and Culture*, ed. David L. Schindler (Notre Dame, Ind.: Our Sunday Visitor, 1990), 98–130 at 114–17, and "Separating Church and State" (see no. 19), and see below chap. 5. It would be amusing to pursue the rather long-term perspective of the Occasional Prayers of the English Missal, which as late as 1963 had the notation under the prayer for the emperor, "Omitted, the Holy Roman Empire being vacant": *The Missal in Latin and English* (Westminster, Md.: Christian Classics, 1963), 205*.

in clear continuity with medieval thought.[21] I wish I had the
space to portray the theory of natural rights and of the principle of subsidiarity aborning in later medieval thought.[22] I
will have to rest content with the observation that knowledge of the almost one thousand years of medieval and modern attention to the question of how temporal and sacral
governments are to be related to one another reveals not just
principles still valid, but perspectives more generous than the
American tradition. An understanding of religious freedom
that does not wrestle with the hope for the world to come,
as set forth in Philippians 2:5–10 and Hebrews 2:6–13 (discussed in the following chapter) that every knee bow at the
name of Christ—and with parallel hopes in other religions—
may have a certain passing attraction, but has not dealt with
half the problem. Of course the hope that "God might be all
in all" has about it an "eschatological" dimension, but as
Karl Rahner insisted, eschatology properly understood is always something that will characterize the next world but
begins in this world.[23] Therefore it is a clue to the direction
in which we should strive. Presumably in America we will
continue to live in a political culture that at the first step,
that is, in the First Amendment, tries to prevent giving the
form of Christ to the world. But this does not mean that a
sober discussion of the principles articulated in the wake of

[21] In addition to Olsen, "Separating Church and State", see "Religion, Politics, and America at the Millennium", *Faith and Reason* 22 (1996): 285–315.

[22] Glenn W. Olsen, "Unity, Plurality, and Subsidiarity in Twentieth Century Context", *Actas del III Congreso "Cultura Europea"* (Pamplona, Spain: Thomas Aranzadi, 1996), 311–17.

[23] Cf. Joseph Ratzinger, *The Spirit of the Liturgy*, trans. John Saward (San
Francisco: Ignatius Press, 2000), 192–93; and David L. Schindler, "Toward a
Culture of Life: The Eucharist, the 'Restoration' of Creation, and the 'Worldly'
Task of the Laity in Liberal Societies", *Communio* 29 (2002): 279–90 at 280.

the Gregorian reform, and a comparison of them to the principles of our own polity, would not be a valuable instrument of cultural criticism.

There is more to be said about Gregory's role in the secularization of European life. André Vauchez has presented Gregory's as an unknowing formulation "of an autonomous secular society", but this begs all kinds of questions.[24] Theocratic monarchy by its self-understanding as under God but above all else had always claimed an innerworldly autonomy: that is, theocratic monarchy had been sacral but normally autonomous in regard to the Church. It had, as in the person of Charlemagne, more commonly supervised the Church than been supervised by it. What Gregory did was to try to free the Church from such supervision, so that she could live her own life. In the degree that he fostered the idea that the goals of the state are temporal and finite, he fostered its secularization. His intent was to reduce the German ruler to holding an office merely of this world. What issued, however, was something more complicated.

Gregory did not give the kingly and imperial powers their first autonomy, but actually tried to do the reverse, effectively to submit them to the judgment of the Church. They were in the future to govern by their own best lights, but under the eye of the Church hierarchy as well as of God. Gregory claimed, not the Church's right to govern temporal matters, but to intervene in them when kings or emperors failed in their obedience to the laws of God. So there is an irony here. The Gregorian attempt to limit the autonomy of sacral theocratic monarchy was met with new theocratic

---

[24] André Vauchez, *The Spirituality of the Medieval West: From the Eighth to the Twelfth Century*, trans. Colette Friedlander (Kalamazoo, Mich.: Cistercian Publications, 1993), 79.

claims: many are unaware that the very term *Holy Roman Empire* was formulated by Frederick I Barbarossa (1152– 1190) as a part of the empire striking back against the papacy. Against papal claims to judge secular rulers, Frederick asserted that he got his authority directly from God, and God alone could judge him.

On the one hand, though the empire fought back at every step, in the very long run—far beyond Henry VIII and Elizabeth I—the days of lay theocracy were numbered— unless one considers theocracy merely disguised in the modern period in, say, the figure of a Joseph II, Holy Roman Emperor from 1765 to 1790, who of course continued to dominate the Church. On the other hand, the cities and the development of commerce rapidly expanding from the eleventh century spawned ever new forms of emancipation that, instead of accepting a diminished understanding of the place of this or that interest group in the world, fought for a world completely in one's own control. In the twelfth century, this might express itself in the communal movement, in the thirteenth in the quest of the arts faculty at Paris for autonomy, or in the fourteenth by the attempt of a city to take over the control of education or welfare from the Church. Even if little of this can be directly attributed to Gregory's program, who can doubt the great secularization of life Gregory in some degree precipitated? The counterpoint is that he also precipitated that relative liberation of the Church by which, instead of being regularly under the thumb of this or that secular ruler, its claims had to be taken seriously. In the twelfth century a charismatic religious figure such as Saint Bernard could face down rulers of all kinds. Though the state was to dominate the modern period, its claims received a kind of limitation in the idea that the hierarchy could be the defender of Christian interests, that is, of the interests of Christendom as a whole, not of simply this or that national state.

Many social and economic factors were at work, and of course no twelfth-century person called any of this secularization, either to praise or to blame it. Still, the many criticisms of commercial and urban life voiced by monk and bishop were in effect an expression of concern about how certain aspects of lay life were being emancipated from Christian influence. Especially in Italy, and especially in population centers where bishops had been the traditional lords, the cry "commune" went out. A commune was a secret mercantile brotherhood sworn, by force if necessary, to wrest control of a city from its traditional lord, whether lay noble or bishop. In city after city from the late eleventh century, bishops were relatively marginalized, and lay forces took greater control.[25] This was a secularization that Gregory VII, only a few years earlier, could hardly have anticipated, though one could argue that in long perspective the forcing of bishops from temporal government observed the logic of the Gregorian position. (The question was very complicated, because many of these bishops had been put into office by one kind of layman, a king, and were now driven out of office by another kind of layman, a merchant.) The entire process raises once again the question of what proper secularization looks like. One is hardly ever disappointed if he takes the low view of humanity and sees much of this on all sides as driven by greed and envy.[26] But much of it also expressed a kind of

---

[25] Miller, *Bishop's Palace*, very effectively portrays the bishops' loss of temporal power and attempts to compensate for this by building programs competing with the communes for urban visual dominance.

[26] One eagerly awaits the second volume of Richard Newhauser, *The Early History of Greed: The Sin of Avarice in Early Medieval Thought and Literature* (New

adolescence, a striking out on one's own and search for some degree of autonomy from some traditional father figure. Like adolescence, it is not intrinsically something to be disapproved, but simply a part of life, something necessary if maturation is to occur.

The growth of the European economy, cities, and a profit mentality from the eleventh century presented Christianity many problems. The old order, centered on monasticism and a rural or village life, saw little to praise and much to condemn in these developments. The old aristocratic order had thought that *noblesse oblige*, but increasingly acquisition seemed to be life's goal. The *Luxuria* figures, sculptures of naked women representing sensual temptation that pepper twelfth-century Romanesque churches, were but one moralizing response to growing fear that increasing prosperity spelled moral decline.[27] Christ had said that where one's wealth was there was one's heart, and by such a standard the merchant seemed to have set his sights on this world rather than the next. The most spectacular rejection of the new life ordered to making money came in the thirteenth century in Saint Francis' turning on his merchant father.[28]

We have seen that all through the early Middle Ages monasticism had often been countercultural, and it had been

---

York: Cambridge University Press, 2000). The first volume goes through the Carolingian period and is a very useful compendium of Christian attitudes toward property. In its epilogue it looks forward to avarice as the dominant vice of the money economy emerging in the period following 1000.

[27] I have discussed a range of meanings these figures possessed in "On the Frontiers of Eroticism: The Romanesque Monastery of San Pedro de Cervatos", *Mediterranean Studies* 8 (1999): 89–104.

[28] Kenneth Baxter Wolf, *The Poverty of Riches: St. Francis of Assisi Reconsidered* (New York: Oxford University Press, 2002), explores the meanings of poverty in Francis' day and the ironies of its spiritual discipline.

common for the monk or nun to take up the life of religion in protest against the manner of life of father or family. Francis' rejection of his father in favor of his bishop retold a story as old as Christ's preaching of the Kingdom—a new family based not on blood but on doing the will of God. Still, as depicted in a great Giotto fresco in the recently damaged and now restored upper church at Assisi, Francis' rejection of his father was particularly radical. Having rejected his father's notion that he should go into the family firm, Francis, in the presence of the bishop of Assisi, stripped himself of all his clothes so that he could return to his father everything he had received from him. Francis would in the future adhere only to Lady Poverty. In spite of his delight in the creation itself, the new world forming spoke to him at every step of danger and temptation to infidelity.

We all know the general outlines of the story. The economic recovery beginning about 1000 clearly brought great benefits. The second millennium of the Christian era has seen much more economic expansion than contraction, and the future was already visible in that amazing 25 percent growth in population that took place between 1150 and 1200.[29] It is not just that in the high Middle Ages prosperity spread and life became more stable and predictable. For many the city improved what we now call the quality of life. Monasteries had been able in a rural environment to nurture a few lives, but in all kinds of ways cities not merely improved the conditions of economic life, but also nurtured the spirit. In cities the pace of life quickened, the range of opportunity broadened, and human intelligence was displayed in greater

---

[29] Glenn W. Olsen, "Marriage in Barbarian Kingdom and Christian Court: Fifth through Eleventh Centuries", in *Christian Marriage: A Historical Study*, ed. Glenn W. Olsen (New York: Herder and Herder, 2001), 146–212 at 183.

variety, especially in urban architecture and that most distinctive of urban products, the university.

Was then the mutual suspicion of monk and merchant misconceived? It is true but superficial to note that the old order, rooted in a rural economy, took a self-protective stance. The issues have not gone away, and the substance of the monks' charges remains with us.[30] Unless we are to dismiss out of hand the whole biblical and patristic tradition in regard to specific matters as usury, more generally in regard to a proper use of wealth, the criticisms raised against the cities and commerce by monk and bishop will always prick sensitive hearts, as is shown by the quest for Islamic banking in our own day—that is, for a way to remain faithful to religious tradition and God in a world gone commercial.[31] Who could deny that, then or now, the cities gave rein to new possibilities for sin, as well as for human flourishing? Just a half-century ago C. S. Lewis, writing from Oxford, from dreamland, still could wonder whether Christians had been unfaithful in not adhering to the proscription of usury. Lewis was not well informed in the matter and apparently was not familiar with Aquinas' distinction between interest and usury, but at least his soul had not been deadened in the manner of Matthew's rich young man, who, hearing Jesus ask him to give up his property, walked away. The high Middle Ages saw the origin of a great debate that, for those whose consciences are not deadened, will not go away. The

---

[30] André Vauchez, *Spirituality*, 75–78. Among Vauchez's other books, see also *Sainthood in the Later Middle Ages* (Cambridge, Eng.: Cambridge University Press, 1997).

[31] Sara Lipton, *Images of Intolerance: The Representation of Jews and Judaism in the Bible Moralisée* (Berkeley, Calif.: University of California Press, 1999), 45, has interesting things to say about moneylending as a "Jewish" activity: see also David Nirenberg, "Conversion, Sex, and Segregation: Jews and Christians in Medieval Spain", *The American Historical Review* 107 (2002): 1065–93 at 1086–87.

cities clearly presented great opportunities for both good and evil, and taking their measure is a task in which we are still engaged. On the one side was a rise in living standards, security, and artificed beauty, on the other a growth in luxury and specific resistance to the Church.[32]

That secularization cannot be conceived as necessarily bad or necessarily good, but more commonly is both at once in a manner that stands in the way of all theories of human progress, becomes manifest in another kind of secularization taking place in twelfth- and thirteenth-century schools and thought.[33] This, the second of the three interrelated developments of interest in the present chapter, is usually described broadly as part of the Renaissance (of learning) of the twelfth century or more narrowly as a dimension of the appearance of scholasticism or of "medieval humanism".[34] Using the latter expression, R. W. Southern was one of the most eloquent spokesmen for its enduring value.[35] In his usage, this humanism was the expansion of rational investigation into all areas of life, without denial that revelation completes our understanding of the natural world.[36]

---

[32] Vauchez, *Spirituality*, 80, 112–14.

[33] The present book aside, Glenn W. Olsen, "Problems with the Contrast between Circular and Linear Views of Time in the Interpretation of Ancient and Early Medieval History", *Fides quaerens intellectum* 1 (2001): 41–65, is my most recent attempt to explore the inadequacy of progressive understandings of history.

[34] Glenn W. Olsen, "Humanism: The Struggle to Possess a Word", to be published in *Logos: A Journal of Catholic Thought and Culture*, will consider the limitations of such terminology.

[35] See his Introduction to R. W. Southern, *Scholastic Humanism and the Unification of Europe*, 1: *Foundations* (Cambridge, Mass.: Blackwell, 1995). Edward Grant, *God and Reason in the Middle Ages* (New York: Cambridge University Press, 2001), is a splendid exploration of medieval intellectual achievement.

[36] See the review of Southern's book by James K. Farge in *Theological Studies* 57 (1996): 747–49. Steven P. Marrone, *The Light of Thy Countenance: Science and Knowledge of God in the Thirteenth Century*, 1: *A Doctrine of Divine Illumination*;

We may deal with this revival of learning much more briefly than we have the increasing incarnationalism and attendant secularization of politics resulting from the quest for a rightly ordered Christian society that has thus far been at the center of this chapter.

Between 1120 and 1140 a group of writers, including Bernard of Chartres, wrote various cosmological works with certain common themes. God was pictured as sufficiently withdrawing from the world after creation to let man subdue it and discover its order. As in the distinction between a sacrament and a sacramental, developing at just this time, the world was disenchanted both so that study of it could proceed, but also so that Christianity could more clearly be distinguished from magic, the specifically Christian from the vaguely numinous. A new balance between grace and nature was struck, one expression of which was the refusal of the Church at the Fourth Lateran Council of 1215 any longer to allow a cleric to participate in ordeals, such as the proof of guilt or innocence by burning hot iron. (If an accused person could briefly hold a piece of hot iron without the resultant burn festering, he had proved his innocence.) Here the Church was on the side of secularization, for ordeals had placed the judgment of cases directly in God's hands. By saying that law cases were to be decided by a more rational process, the Church took the side of Bernard of Chartres and agreed that man lived in a sufficiently intelligible *saeculum* that not every matter had to be thrown back into God's hands.[37]

Bernard is not usually numbered among the scholastics, but his attitude to the world was in considerable measure shared

---

2: *God at the Core of Cognition*, 2 vols. (Leiden, Netherlands: Brill, 2001), a demanding work, represents the current state of scholarship.

[37] Vauchez, *Spirituality*, 79–80.

by them and led to their exploration of how much a systematic human knowledge of the world is possible. Again we have gain and loss. As writers as different as Jean Leclercq and Hans Urs von Balthasar have noted, in scholasticism we gain clarity about the world and orderliness in its study, but commonly at the expense of older patristic and monastic approaches, which were less taken with *disputatio* for its own sake and more interested in the actual appropriation of Scripture into one's life.[38] There was a tendency for a theology issuing from prayer and meditation on Scripture to be replaced by one issuing from book study. Though in both cases the object of reflection was God, in the former the goal was weighted toward experience of God, in the latter toward understanding him. The patristic and monastic approach involved intimacy, the scholastic a certain distancing or objectivity. The clarity and self-consciousness of scholasticism were real advances, but at the same time represented loss and a certain kind of secularization. The same may be said of the growing place of quantification in life about this time. Who can deny that visualizing the universe increasingly in quantitative terms during the high Middle Ages did not represent an advance of thought? This advance was to generate its own problems, but the secularization of the world caused by increasingly attempting to quantify it did allow the formation of kinds of knowledge hardly previously dreamed of.[39]

[38] This is a recurrent theme in von Balthasar's writings when he takes up scholasticism. It also is a *leitmotiv* in Leclercq's *The Love of Learning and the Desire for God: A Study of Monastic Culture*, trans. Catherine Misrahi, 3rd ed. (New York: Fordham University Press, 1982).

[39] Alfred W. Crosby, *The Measure of Reality: Quantification and Western Society, 1250–1600* (Cambridge, England: Cambridge University Press, 1996). For the argument that there is a direct linkage between the development of Catholic theology and the development of science, see Peter E. Hodgson, "The Christian Origin of Science", *Logos* 4, no. 2 (2001): 138, and Stanley L.

If at Paris there was an intellectual precision simply un-
available in medieval society before the thirteenth century,
this precision went in tandem with other less desirable developments beyond decrease in piety. There was, for instance, in the new universities a second kind of distancing,
this time of student from professor, and diminishment of the
personal form of education attendant on the imitation of the
character of living masters found in the cathedral schools of
earlier centuries. What happens in one area of life regularly
impacts others, and C. Stephen Jaeger argues that the shift
from a culture built around real presence, that is, the "real
presence" of a living master, to one built around symbolic
presence presented and presents a real problem for the Real
Presence.[40] Can the doctrine of the Real Presence survive
in a culture become rationalist? Is there some meaningful
sense in which we, looking back on these developments, can
discover better ways in which the new rationalism could have
been synthesized with what was good about the prescholas-
tic world? More generally, is there some better way than we
have discovered of preserving the old, each age as we leave
it, as we develop the new? Must we always oscillate between
one unbalanced view of life and another? I have partly addressed these questions in the first chapter and would answer
here in the same spirit. What was desirable was not that all
cosmological or "precritical" thinking be abandoned, but re-
tention, for instance, by way of the liturgy, of a cosmological
framework within which to place the growing precisions of
science.

Jaki, *A Mind's Matter: An Intellectual Autobiography* (Grand Rapids, Mich.: W. B.
Eerdmans, 2002).

[40] *The Envy of Angels: Cathedral Schools and Social Ideals in Medieval Europe,
950–1200* (Philadelphia: University of Pennsylvania Press, 1994), 164, 190.

Something similar may be said in the matter of miracles and claims to sanctity at this time. In contrast to the Roman period, in the early Middle Ages, a time when blood and descent counted so much, the saint had been most commonly portrayed as born or predestined to sanctity. Royal and aristocratic saints abounded. (For example, in the sixth century Venantius Fortunatus wrote the life of the ex-queen Radegund, who with her daughter had become a nun. In the seventh century both Saint Eligius of Noyon and the writer of his life, Dado of Rouen, had been among the chief councilors of the King.) In the twelfth century, by contrast, something like the late Roman perspective returned, and saints and sanctity were thought to be forged by choices, ascetic discipline, and the practice of charity. Finally Innocent III declared that miracles are valid only when supported by a holy life and by witnesses. Sanctity becomes something itself subject to verification by reason. It perhaps is an acceptable paradox to speak of a licit secularization of the sacred, in which reason was used to prune away magic and whimsy to let a genuine holiness stand forth.[41]

There were other aspects to the growth of incarnationalism beyond exploration of the possibility of reordering political life by Christian principles. Medieval writers loved to characterize the world's history as composed of various ages. Were we to do this, the period beginning with Saint Anselm in the late eleventh century could be called the age of Christ, or of the humanity or Incarnation of Christ.[42] Perhaps the

---

[41] Vauchez, *Spirituality*, 149–50.

[42] Of my various writings on Anselm, see "St. Anselm's Place in Hans Urs von Balthasar's History of Soteriology", in *Cur Deus Homo*, ed. Paul Gilbert, Helmut Kohlenberger, and Elmar Salmann (*Studia Anselmiana*, 128; Rome: Centro Studi S. Anselmo, 1999), 823–35. For the Incarnation in the art of this

most developed and spectacular expression of this, made famous in two much debated books of Leo Steinberg, ultimately was the insistence of many Renaissance painters on
Christ's sexuality, on insisting through the depiction of gen-
itals and circumcision that he was fully a sexual being.[43] Things
are rarely simple, and Christ as Judge continued to dominate
in the tympana of twelfth-century churches, but in piety and
devotion the emphasis increasingly was on the love revealed
in the Incarnation, God's sharing of the human condition,
suffering, and death for man. Thus the third interrelated development of this chapter, the growth of affective piety and
subjectivity in religion, of identification with this love, suffering, and death of Jesus.[44] Note that this was often not on
the same track as the development of scholasticism and could
be part of another current or of a countercurrent. At the
level of popular devotion, each subsequent medieval century
would more and more identify with the suffering Jesus.[45]

period, see Jean Wirth, *L'Image à l'Époque Romane* (Paris: Éditions du Cerf,
1999), 329–450, esp. 362–78.

[43] *The Sexuality of Christ in Renaissance Art and in Modern Oblivion*, 2nd ed.
(Chicago: University of Chicago Press, 1996), and *Leonardo's Incessant Last Supper* (New York: Zone Books, 2001).

[44] In studies such as "Christian Perfection and *transitus ad monasterium* in
Lupus of Ferrières' Letter 29", in *Proceedings of the Eighth International Congress
of Medieval Canon Law*, University of California, San Diego, Aug. 20–27, 1988
(*Monumenta iuris canonici, series C: Subsidia*, vol. 9, Vatican City: Biblioteca Apostolica Vaticana, 1991), 355–68, and "One Heart and One Soul (Acts 4:32 and
34) in Dhuoda's *Manual*", *Church History* 61 (1992): 23–33, I have noted that
we find a measure of these developments already in the Carolingian period.
See Celia Chazelle, *The Crucified God in the Carolingian Era: Theology and Art of
Christ's Passion* (Cambridge, Eng.: Cambridge University Press, 2001), and the
overview of the early Middle Ages in Thomson, *Western Church in the Middle
Ages*, 76–77.

[45] See Ellen M. Ross, *The Grief of God: Images of the Suffering Jesus in Late
Medieval England* (New York: Oxford University Press, 1997), the typically

It is very important to understand how such a development came to ask more and more of human beings. When, as in the early Middle Ages, God or Christ was presented as Judge and Cosmocrator, God and man were imagined in a relationship something like king and subject. This partially accounts for a certain formalism—as I have already argued, not in itself necessarily a bad thing—which some have espied in early medieval spirituality, which even in its highest, monastic, forms tended to ask conformity of the individual in service of splendid, disciplined, communal worship. The proper human responses were veneration and praise, but one hardly thought of imitation of such an awesome being. This was still probably the dominant experience of Christianity at the beginning of the twelfth century and helps us account for the popularity of such ritual or objective or external acts of worship as pilgrimage and crusade, which can easily involve more a piety of the body than of the soul. (A piety of an integrated body and soul is not ruled out.) As emphasis began to shift in the eleventh century to St. Paul's view that Christ was as us in all things but sin—that is, to the idea that he had lived a human life with all its opportunities and temptations—his life became available for imitation in ways it had not been earlier. Thus arose the great interest in imitating that life as found in the Gospels or in returning to the life of the first Christians.[46] Such interest could hardly miss

brilliant essay of Caroline Bynum, "The Blood of Christ in the Later Middle Ages", *Church History* 71 (2002): 685–714, and Rachel Fulton, *From Judgment to Passion: Devotion to Christ and the Virgin Mary 800–1200* (New York: Columbia University Press, 2002). See also Thomas H. Bestul, *Texts of the Passion: Latin Devotional Literature and Medieval Society* (Philadelphia: University of Pennsylvania Press, 1996).

[46] My most recent study of imitation of the life of the first Christians will orient the reader to scholarship on this theme from the late Roman world

Christ's concern over neighbor as well as God, and imitation
of his life led to new concerns, especially with the poor.
These are no better summarized than in the life of Saint
Francis.[47]

But arguably the greatest advance here was that reflection
on the life of Christ led to thinking of oneself as having a
personal calling. In the early Middle Ages, most people hardly
had an internal life. Were it not for the fact that early medieval peoples came from cultures in which there had never
been much place for the personal, the splendid objective communal worship expressed above all in the monasteries, but at
a more modest level also in the parish, could be spoken of as
having been an obstacle to the development of their interior
life. In its own setting it probably was, rather, a means by
which formerly barbarian peoples' sights were raised to think
of the greatness of God. Now, from the eleventh century,
people increasingly asked what demands the life of Christ
put on them, what Christ was asking of them. They saw
themselves less as members of a group and more as individuals before God.

Some have seen in this the discovery of the individual,
and certainly the twelfth century was central to the formation of that emphasis on the individual that was to become
distinctive of a large sweep of Western civilization, only now
in our own day receding in the face of the anonymity and
lack of self-consciousness encouraged by mass technological
culture. Indeed, one of the strange ways we are linked to

---

through the Reformation: "The *Ecclesia Primitiva* in John Cassian, the Ps. Jer-
ome Commentary on Mark, and Bede", in *Biblical Studies in the Early Middle
Ages*, ed. Michael Gorman and Claudio Leonardi (Florence: SISMEL Edizioni
del Galuzzo, 2004), 3–25.

[47] Vauchez, *Spirituality*, 84–89, 145–48.

high medieval culture is that we seem in our day to be returning to what preceded it, that is, because we know so little history and have been so formed by an education aimed at facilitating technological civilization, returning in some respects to a timeless and objective civilization with some similarities to the early Middle Ages, more an oral than a written culture. Our times are becoming increasingly timeless in the sense that so few now have a knowledge of history that most lack a clear sense of where they or their civilization stand in history: they belong to no story or history. The civilization is becoming more and more objective in the sense that fewer and fewer have a rich interior life or a sense of their own distinctiveness, and increasingly one's norms are absorbed from cyberspace.[48]

In the twelfth century modes of religious life proliferated, each trying, not simply to recover the first form of Christian life, but to find the most appropriate way of serving God at the present. This seems to have been related to the increasing dissatisfaction with the world as it is and interest in changing it broadcast in the Gregorian reform. In the early Middle Ages, the world and its present structures had been accepted as divinely decreed. Now increasingly a restlessness filled the

[48] See my "St. Augustine and the Problem of the Medieval Discovery of the Individual", *Word and Spirit: A Monastic Review* 9 (1987): 129–56, with Vauchez, *Spirituality*, 153–62. Aidan Nichols, "Zion and Philistia: The Liturgy and Theological Aesthetics Today", a lecture summarized in "A Summary of Papers Presented at the 1996 Society for Catholic Liturgy Conference, 'Liturgy and Beauty' ", in *Antiphon: Publication of the Society for Catholic Liturgy* 1, nos. 2/3 (Fall/Winter 1996): 14–16 at 16, is described as citing "Taylor Forsyth's observation that it is improbable that a great Christian art will arise once more 'till the condition of its existence in the Middle Ages is again realized, and we possess a theology which is not only tolerated by the public intelligence, but is welcome for life, commanding for the reason, and fascinating for the imagination of the age'." There may be a long wait.

spiritual life, in which discrepancies between ideal and reality were to be challenged. Again, the lives of Saints Francis and Dominic, active in the world, witness this new sensibility. It is not just that what may loosely be called lay spirituality was being born, but an incarnational spirituality trying in a busy life to order all things to God. The place in Christian consciousness of contemplation was receding, and action was increasingly seen as a value. Thomas Aquinas was ultimately to declare that all contemplation must be ordered to action. This had ramifications for many subjects, not least the ongoing reevaluation of work.[49]

Incarnational and lay spirituality developed in tandem. Little corresponding to a "theology or spirituality of the laity" had existed before Gregory VII's day. But the great struggle between Gregory and Henry involved ideas, some of which were not that difficult to understand. German bishops and nobles had had to take sides, for or against the good old German theocratic way of doing things, or for or against the papal notion of right order. The struggle between Pope and king became a matter of passionate dispute, and from this time the consciousness of Europe was raised about matters of Christian obligation. Gregory, desperate for a power base, had resorted to appeals to laymen to turn against corrupt priests and had even sanctioned the use of force. In a general sense, the flourishing of religion in so many forms in the twelfth century, the impact that a figure like Saint Bernard (1090–1153) could make on his times, all followed in the wake of Gregory VII's profound disturbing of conventional assumptions about Christian society.

---

[49] In this paragraph I am recasting Vauchez, *Spirituality*, 87–89, 98–99, 122–27 (on the reevaluation of work).

In 1075 Gregory anticipated both the Crusades and one possible form a lay spirituality might take, the knight with his strong arm and sword placed in the cause of justice and the Church.[50] Calling Christians to defense of their brethren in the East against Turkish oppression, Gregory wrote, "Let some of you who are willing to defend the Christian faith come, fight for your heavenly King. If God will, we will make preparations so that all who are willing to cross the sea with us may defend the nobility of heaven, and be not afraid to show they are sons of God."[51] In the event, Gregory became preoccupied with other problems, and it was to be another twenty years before Pope Urban II called the "armed pilgrimage" that we now refer to as the First Crusade. Surprising enough, the call to crusade was answered not just by knights, but also by thousands from all levels of society. By 1100 laymen were increasingly receptive to the adventure of being Christian and, in search of a spiritual life of their own, sought ways of being Christian in the world. Increasingly, we see them involved in the great flowering of charitable institutions that from the 1100s blanketed Europe with hospitals, schools, hospices, and leper houses, as well as bridge- and highway-building confraternities, orders to ransom Christian prisoners and slaves from the

---

[50] For an example of the kind of intelligent revisionism shaking Crusade studies, which tends now to read the Crusades not as an early stage of European imperialism but as a "peace-keeping mission" or exercise in "liberation theology", see Jonathan Riley-Smith, *What Were the Crusades?* 3rd ed. (San Francisco: Ignatius Press, 2002).

[51] Register II, 37, trans. Francis Rudolph, "The Crusades: A Clash of Civilizations", *Second Spring: A Journal of Faith and Culture* 2 (2002): 12–19 at 13. I have made some changes in this translation on the basis of the Latin text given in *Quellen zum Investiturstreit*, pt. 1, ed. Franz-Josef Schmale (Darmstadt: Wissenschaftliche Buchgesellschaft, 1978), 138.

Muslims. Early medieval ritualistic ideas of poverty, the feed-
ing of paupers on feast days or the obligation of monasteries
in the Benedictine tradition to support twelve poor men,
increasingly gave way before the idea that poverty should be
directly combated and contact with the poor be direct.[52] As
great as Saint Francis' special witness to poverty in the thirteenth century was Count Theobald's response to famine in
1143 in Champagne: he opened his granaries, asked that the
poor be reported to him, and sent out religious to look for
the sick and for lepers. This was one layman's response to
the idea being propagated by preachers and canon lawyers
that almsgiving is a duty for the rich and not just a super-
erogatory act of charity.[53]

Gregory VII's challenge to the conventional assumptions
about Christian society and Urban II's attempt to involve all
society in the liberation of the Holy Land, along with more
general pastoral work to stir up the laity to increased appropriation of Christianity, had a great impact on the most common form of the lay state, marriage. Still in the year 1100, a
heavy weight of misogyny and suspicion of all things carnal
weighed down learned opinion about marriage. A popular-
ized Augustinianism associated all sexual life with sin. In this
view intercourse was always at least a venial sin and was to be
undergone reluctantly and with a certain amount of embar-
rassment. In the mid-eleventh century Peter Damian had illustrated the proper attitude by speaking of the elephant,

---

[52] Jutta Maria Berger, *Die Geschichte der Gastfreundschaft im hochmittelalterli-
chen Mönchtum: Die Cistercienser* (Berlin: Akademie Verlag, 1999), in spite of its
title, deals with all aspects of the practice of charity by many high medieval
religious orders. Cf. Daniel Le Blévec, *La part du pauvre: L'assistance dans les
pays du Bas-Rhône du XIIe siècle au milieu du XVe siècle*, preface by Georges
Duby, 2 vols. (Rome: École française de Rome, 2000), on a single region.

[53] Vauchez, *Spirituality*, 104–35, 131–34.

which, "impelled to the act of propagation, turns its head away, showing thereby that it is acting under compulsion from nature, against its will, and that it is ashamed and disgusted at what it is doing".[54] Throughout the twelfth century, monks and priests attempted to adjust such views, to reconsider marriage as a possible path to saintliness. Pope Alexander III (1159–1181) marked a decisive stage of development here when, in a letter to the master of the Knights of Saint James, he attempted to end an old controversy about the states of perfection, writing that married knights could be considered religious in a canonical sense and stating explicitly that virginity was not necessary to perfection.

Some modern Scripture scholars and theologians maintain that Christ never intended to set up a hierarchy of states of life or perfection, that his emphasis was on the radical conversion of all.[55] However this may be, before the thirteenth century this—the idea that the Gospel radically calls all—had been an exceptional view, found perhaps in Saint Basil's call to "complete Christianity".[56] But in 1253 the great canonist Henry of Susa declared for this minority report, now perhaps echoed in the teachings of Vatican II, by stating that the term *religious* did not describe a canonical state of life, but "in a broad sense, those persons are called religious who live in a saintly and religious manner in their homes,

---

[54] Vauchez, *Spirituality*, 115–16, at 116 for the quotation.

[55] Such a perspective pervades the chapter "Marriage in the New Testament", by Francis Martin in Olsen, ed., *Christian Marriage*, 50–100, and then is traced in my own following chapter, "Progeny, Faithfulness, Sacred Bond: Marriage in the Age of Augustine", 101–45. Such a view is central to the thought of Hans Urs von Balthasar. For what precedes and follows, see Vauchez, *Spirituality*, 127, 130.

[56] Olsen, "Progeny, Faithfulness, Sacred Bond", in *Christian Marriage*, ed. Olsen, 101.

not because they submit to a specific rule, but on account of their life, which is harder and simpler than that of other lay people who live in a purely worldly fashion".[57] We have now, arguably, with Henry of Susa returned to the Gospel viewpoint, in which, in Vauchez' words, "religious life is not a state but a lifestyle".[58] I would also note—and Hostiensis catches this up in his idea that the life of the religious layman is harder and simpler than the life of other laymen—that a plausible sense of the way (or one way) the layman might be in, but not of, the world had formed by the thirteenth century. However, even though the Fourth Lateran Council had declared marriage one of the seven sacraments in 1215, we are at the end of our period still far from the fully developed spirituality of marriage of Saint Francis de Sales, and we are also far from the understanding that marriage is as much a specifically chosen vocation as celibacy.

The pursuit of more personal religion and radical Christianity could not escape the ambiguity of all human achievement. To take the Cistercians as an example, the order's greatest writers, Saint Bernard of Clairvaux, William of Saint Thierry, or Aelred of Rievaulx, took the exploration of man's union with God to new heights, but often at the expense of a radical contempt for the world, which in Bernard's case included contempt for the new world of scholarship and human capacity his contemporary Bernard of Chartres was extolling. The Cistercians present the dilemma, played out again and again in the history of religion, of how much criticism

[57] Vauchez, *Spirituality*, 142, for this and the following quotation. There is another translation of this passage and parallel discussion in André Vauchez, *The Laity in the Middle Ages: Religious Beliefs and Devotional Practices*, ed. Daniel E. Bornstein, trans. Margery J. Schneider (Notre Dame, Ind.: University of Notre Dame Press, 1993), 113–14.

[58] Ibid.

coming from the side of religion any society can bear, even understand. It is the question of the hard sayings of Jesus himself, against which are ranged the suasive arguments of the Grand Inquisitor.

L. Genicot observed of the twelfth century that spiritual demands increased as economic necessity grew less stringent.[59] By this he meant that the objectivity, conformism, and lack of the personal in early medieval society were related to the hardness of the times, to most people living at a subsistence level. The deepening individualism, subjectivity, and assimilation of Christianity of the twelfth century were likewise some of the luxuries made possible by a growing economy. Such generalization can be doubted. A good case could be made for the reverse argument, that difficult circumstances make people ask more of themselves. In our times, for instance, it seems as if those who have had to work under great constraints, the Polish church under communism or the hidden Church of China today, manifest the most striking religious life, and those in prosperous civilizations are the ones who have become spiritually banal. Probably the lesson to be drawn is that it is not possible to generalize about claimed linkages between material circumstance and spiritual development. Better the views of a Chesterton (in *Orthodoxy*) or of a Christopher Dawson, who, looking directly at the history of the Church in our period, found in it a spiritual ferment so pervasive that they could claim that it had come to characterize the entire civilization, differentiating it from those cultures that had never been disturbed by the questions posed by Gregory VII.[60] What is right in such

---

[59] Vauchez, *Spirituality*, 163–64, reflects on Genicot.

[60] This argument is found in many of Christopher Dawson's books, but see especially *Progress and Religion*, published in a new edition with a foreword by

views is not so much that they reverse a common perspective in which economic and technological change are seen as the motors of cultural dynamism, as that they insist on the dynamic centrality of the role religion has played from biblical times.[61]

Christina Scott and an introduction by Mary Douglas (Washington, D.C.: Catholic University of America Press, 2001). Caroline Walker Bynum, *Metamorphosis and Identity* (New York: Zone Books, 2001), explores many forms of the twelfth- and early thirteenth-century preoccupation with change.

[61] I am slightly reformulating a point made by Robert Royal, "Dawson's History: Resurrecting the Work of Christopher Dawson", in *The Weekly Standard* (Mar. 17, 2003): 33–35 at 35.

IV

The Church in the World from Renaissance to Enlightenment

What did it mean in the early modern European world to find God in all things and do all to the greater glory of God? This question resonates of the sixteenth century, embodying as it does the two most famous Jesuit mottoes of the Catholic Reformation. But it also embodies a discussion as old as Christianity about the value of the world and the place and purpose of the Christian therein. The broad outlines of this discussion have been anticipated in previous chapters and are the following. The earliest Christian centuries were of uncertain mind in regard to the mode of the presence of God in all things. On the one hand, God the Creator had made all and was in some sense in everything. Still, the world seemed to be in the power of Satan.[1] Consequently, the Christian had to be a *miles Christi*, a soldier of Christ, fighting to push back Satan's dominion; this was especially the self-understanding of the first monks.[2]

Early Christians also were uncertain as to exactly how all is to be done to God's glory. Certainly, after Constantine's

[1] Gerard E. Caspary, *Politics and Exegesis: Origen and the Two Swords* (Berkeley, Calif.: University of California Press, 1979), nicely teases out the tension between these claims.

[2] Mathew Kuefler, *The Manly Eunuch: Masculinity, Gender Ambiguity, and Christian Ideology in Late Antiquity* (Chicago: University of Chicago Press, 2001), 105–24.

conversion, great public statements or representations of the glory of God were made, as in the mosaics of the churches of Rome. But the very conversion of the emperor raised in an acute form the question of whether the world was to be captured for Christ in, for instance, some political or cultural order or whether, rather in the manner of the developing icon, God's glory shines into the world not as the sun filling a room, but as a ray of light sharply etched against the darkness. If the latter case, perhaps, the glory of God is most witnessed in the great countercultural deed, the faithfulness of martyr or hermit when others are faithless or cowardly.

In important ways Christians were the heirs of the Jewish tradition of the Psalmist (Psalms 8:5–8), "What is man that thou shouldst remember him? . . . Thou hast placed him only a little below the angels, crowning him with glory and honour, and bidding him rule over the works of thy hands. Thou has put them all under his dominion, the sheep and the cattle, and the wild beasts besides" (Knox translation). Such a view implied that man is the crowning glory of the creation, over which they are intended to rule, and that this creation is splendid. These ideas were at the furthest remove from any turning from or despising of the world. They were taken into Christianity from the first in Ephesians 1:22 and Hebrews 2:6–13, in which Christ as the New Man was said to place all under his dominion. We might label the view thus expressed "early Christian humanism".[3] It stood against all refusal of the world.

---

[3] Glenn W. Olsen, "From Bede to the Anglo-Saxon Presence in the Carolingian Empire", in *Angli e Sassoni al di qua e al di là del mare* (Settimane di studio del Centro italiano di studi sull'alto medioevo, 32; Spoleto, Italy: Centro Italiano di Studi sull'alto Medioevo, 1986), 305–82 at 321–22.

The passage in Hebrews is extraordinary. First, by applying the Psalms text to Christ the New Man, the author of Hebrews makes Christ the norm for the definition of humanity. Christ leads the way in articulating the dominion of men over the world. What is true of him is potentially true of them. Speaking of the world to come, which however begins to form in time, the author of Hebrews says that at present we cannot see that in fact everything has been placed under Christ's command. But because he submitted to death, Christ now is "crowned with glory and splendour" (2:9). Since it was God's goal to bring many to glory, it was appropriate that God perfect through suffering him who would lead his brothers to salvation or sanctification.

The implications in this passage for the Christian assessment of man and the world are immense. Some have been touched on in the last chapter. On the one hand, though human glorification and sanctification and dominion over the world are the goals, eschatological glory and splendor apparently shine only intermittently in this world, which is less than fully obedient to Christ. Because glorification lies only on the other side of suffering or is gained through suffering, in this life we are only working our way to glory. Such a view does not specify the limits of human capacity. Those limits lie open and depend on how much in fact people conform their lives to Christ. Obedience and suffering are central to history, but because these are the means of human perfection, anticipations of glory run throughout human life. Such ideas suggest that though the Christian is always called to a "humanism" following the form of Christ, to a domination of the world that articulates the range of human capacity by helping the world's possibilities emerge, the world, in bondage to evil, mightily resists.

No one in a second-century Christian context under-stood the presence of splendor in human life better than Ire-naeus of Lyons, for whom the glory of God showed forth in the human face and the well-composed body. Irenaeus' view, like that of his younger contemporary Clement of Alexan-dria (c. 150–c. 215), was at the furthest remove from those ascetics who scorned marriage, urban life, and the body. Af-ter the conversion of Constantine, these two tendencies, that of Irenaeus and that of at least many of the ascetics, struggled throughout the late ancient world and the entire Middle Ages. While the empire moved in the direction of at least a formal Christianization of all life, eventually identifying Roman cit-izenship with being Christian, the monks moved to the desert. Views like those of Irenaeus never wholly disappeared and occurred especially commonly in the early medieval schools. Thus C. Stephen Jaeger, as noted in the last chapter, has shown how concerned early medieval education, especially in ca-thedral schools, was to teach good manners, the carriage of one's body, and the arts of ingratiation.[4] Such goals implied that men were not to abandon the world, but to continue to make it a place suited to human life, a place ever more hu-man. The body was the register of the soul and as such was not to be neglected. The goal was the body's harmonious and dignified comportment, desirable not simply morally but also aesthetically.

We have also seen in the last chapter that though the ten-dency to abandon or despair of the world was very powerful in the early Middle Ages, from the eleventh century an in-carnational impulse that held that men are to enter the world and bring forth good things to the glory of God gradually

---

[4] *The Envy of Angels: Cathedral Schools and Social Ideals in Medieval Europe,* 950–1200 (Philadelphia: University of Pennsylvania Press, 1994).

came to the fore. Miguel Ayuso has suggested that man has two irreducible orientations, one vertical and one horizontal.[5] We can label the former theocentric or eschatological, for in it man is defined in relation to God; and the latter humanistic or incarnational, for in it man realizes himself by the worldly exercise of his freedom, always of course in the Christian view in obedience to God. Development of the former orientation had been the special interest of monasticism and the early Middle Ages. Now from the eleventh century interest turned increasingly to pursuit of the second, horizontal, orientation. Arguably, though the vertical relation with God is ultimately more important both for salvation and for understanding man in his depths, and from a Christian point of view neither orientation is to be detached from the other, it is in the exercise of freedom in shaping the world in their horizontal relations to other men and things that men normally exercise their vocations.[6] What we might say, therefore, is that increasingly from the eleventh century interest shifted toward exploring this-worldly life in all its social, political, and historical dimensions. Christian humanism can be described as pursuit of these goals framed by a Christian understanding of man.

That an incarnational impulse developed from the eleventh century does not mean simply that some form of Christian optimism henceforth came to replace Christian pessimism. Rather, the most perceptive came to see that in some sense both attitudes toward the world, the incarnational and the eschatological, have a hold on truth. Thus in the twelfth century John of Salisbury (c. 1115–1180) insisted that human

---

[5] "Francisco Elias de Tejada en la ciencia juridico-politica hispana", *Anales de la Fundación Francisco Elías de Tejada* 3 (1997): 15–34 at 18.

[6] Ayuso, "Francisco Elias de Tejada", 18.

life is at once exalted and abased.[7] John saw that Christianity is about finding one's life by losing it. That is how Hebrews 2:9 had applied the text of Psalms 8 to Christ: Jesus is crowned with glory "because of the death he underwent". Slowly the issues came into focus. Writers like John came to see elements of what Hans Urs von Balthasar (1905–1988) has in our own day laid bare as an aesthetic distinctive to Christianity, built around two "moments" or "movements" in the life of Christ. The first is descending (*kenosis*) and includes Incarnation, death on the Cross, and the taking on of the sins of the world. The second is ascending (*ascensus*) and includes victory over death, ascent to the Father, and all the themes associated with Christ as *pantocrator*, Lord of the universe.

Commonly, Balthasar observed, the dramatic tensions found in Christian thought about mankind's nature and destiny result from trying to affirm that, as called to imitation of Christ, simultaneously men are abased and glorious, descending and ascending. Although John of Salisbury could not have put it von Balthasar's way, he saw that life was in a profound sense mixed. Augustine (354–430) had already emphasized that in this world the wheat and tares grow together. Through his own bitter experience of exile, John developed a heightened sense of the ways the world is simultaneously open to sin and sanctification and, as the field on which human salvation and definition are being worked out, is at once the dominion of Satan and a witness to God's glory. John saw life neither as tragic in a Greek sense nor as progressive in a modern sense, but as something in which splendor and death are linked to one another.

---

[7] Glenn W. Olsen, "John of Salisbury's Humanism", in *Gli Umanesimi medievali*, ed. Claudio Leonardi (Florence: SISMEL Edizioni del Galluzzo, 1998), 447–68.

By John's day longstanding debate about how human beings are to be defined was being clarified by growing realization that from a Christian point of view, man's body is as
necessary as his soul to human definition. That is, a Platonic
definition of mankind in which man is thought of as essentially soul, rather than as embodied soul, was increasingly
seen as inadequate to Christian understanding. In some respects, as Saint Bernard put it, the disciplined human body is
"the envy of angels".[8] The growing sense that men are as
much their bodies as their souls lay behind increasing appreciation and study of the human body, both in art and in
science. Already in twelfth-century art a longstanding tradition of portrayal of a naked and ashamed Adam and Eve began to be replaced with sensuous, even insouciant, portrayals
of especially Eve (at Moissac or Vezelay, for instance); Gi-
labertus presented Salome in all her seductiveness (at Saint-
Étienne, Toulouse);[9] the heroic male nude returned (at
Frómista); coquetry became a subject in its own right (see
the woman combing her hair before joining her lover at Santa
Maria, L'Estany, Barcelona); and especially the female form
was increasingly revealed through the use of cinched belt
and fitted bodice.[10]

From the fourteenth century the conviction grew that, in
spite of all, the world is a splendid place full of interest and
possibility. *Curiositas*, so vigorously condemned by Augustine, insistently advanced to the fore in the thought of
Petrarch (1304–74), even if yoked to strong suspicion that

---

[8] Jaeger, *Envy of Angels*, vi.

[9] There is a plate in V. A. Kolve, "Ganymede/*Son of Getron*: Medieval
Monasticism and Same-Sex Desire", *Speculum* 73 (1998): 1014–67, fig. 5.

[10] I have prepared a study with plates, "Sex and the Romanesque in Occitania-
Provence", to be published in a festschrift for James Brundage, which will
illustrate these developments.

Augustine had been right. Already in the previous century, Thomas Aquinas' politics had expressed greater confidence in the political enterprise than had those of Augustine. Though humanism of the sort John of Salisbury had embraced died with John's generation, to be replaced by scholasticism, many of John's interests survived transition to a university setting. Thus the development of natural-law thinking and the perception that nature has its own integrity, characteristic of Aquinas' thought, paid the world a homage due it. Such views were to persist and linked the scholastics with the confidence in the laws of nature of the early modern scientists. Recent scholarship rightly insists that, overwhelmingly, in what we have come to call the Renaissance, a rising estimate of and interest in the world continued to be framed within Christian understanding, so that few forgot that man is a sinner. Writers such as Petrarch in the fourteenth century or Pico della Mirandola (1463–1494) in the fifteenth might fairly be described as torn between or existing between worlds, as seeing the truth of what was most somber in the Augustinian view while loving the world and its possibilities.[11]

Undeniably during these centuries a form of secularization took place that especially for certain elite populations replaced God the Lord of creation with something vaguer, less personal, and more remote. As Erwin Panofsky observed, the very development of perspective in Renaissance art tended toward a rejection of medieval religious realism in

---

[11] See Carol Everhart Quillen, *Rereading the Renaissance: Petrarch, Augustine, and the Language of Humanism* (Ann Arbor, Mich.: University of Michigan Press, 1998), and the correction of scholarship already found in Henri de Lubac, *Pic de la Mirandole: études et discussions* (Paris: Aubier Montaigne, 1974).

favor of a kind of objectivity.[12] For some beauty itself, made into either a transcendental or an anthropomorphized Dame Nature, effectively replaced God. Machiavelli (1469–1527) went the furthest and, as the most advanced expression of a restlessness in the matter of God's domination of the world found in some circles around 1500, denied God and providence completely. Historians have been telling us that during these centuries for most people Christianity may actually have come to influence the details of everyday life more than it had in the Middle Ages. But the reformers of the sixteenth century rightly worried whether the world had somehow become separated from God, standing not under Christ's dominion but proudly autonomous.

Both Protestant and Catholic Reforms were attempts to overcome every tendency to sever the world from God. On the Catholic side the goal was to affirm the truth of a medieval perspective in which theology remained the queen of the sciences, that is, in which Christianity remained the ordering principle of human life, while also affirming the truth of Renaissance emphasis on the splendor that shines through the creation and is manifest in human creativity and initiative. The Reign of Christ was to be proclaimed, but not in a manner that suffocated man or obscured his place as cocreator with God. Both Protestant and Catholic Reformations, but above all the Baroque art and architecture eventually spreading from Rome from the late sixteenth century, represented attempts to resacralize a European life that had been,

---

[12] Erwin Panofsky, *Perspective as Symbolic Form*, trans. Christopher S. Wood (New York: Zone Books, 1991), 72, with the discussion in Bruce W. Holsinger, "Medieval Studies, Postcolonial Studies, and the Genealogies of Critique", *Speculum* 77 (2002): 1195–1227 at 1215. In its own way, and in regard to both the medieval and other parts of the world, this article, as at 1217–18, undermines progressive views of history.

from the viewpoint of Christ's dominion, unraveling and, for instance, in the development of an uninhibited commercial life, had been declaring its independence from all external regulation.

The Gregorian reform of the eleventh century had understood that for effective reform of the Church there must be a developed institutional base. This lesson was not lost on the reformers of the sixteenth century. They realized that the ineffectiveness of the programs of many would-be fourteenth- and fifteenth-century reformers had to be laid at the door of insufficient attention to mundane matters and saw that reform had to involve much more than well-intentioned moral proposals. On all sides, Catholic and Protestant also cast about outside ecclesiastical institutional structures for some strong lay or political arm by which to advance the resacralization of society. The large outlines of the story are well known. Luther (1483–1536) turned to the German princes, Calvin (1509–1564) to Geneva, and the Catholics to the Holy Roman Emperor. In terms of our story, from midcentury the Jesuit mottoes alluded to at the beginning of this chapter articulated as never before a campaign not just somehow to reconnect this world to God, but to show how God is in the world. The Christian task on the Catholic side was increasingly understood as aiming at the revelation of the immanent presence of God in all things. Such a task carried its typical temptations, too well understood by our perhaps more democratic age, but on its own terms continued the exploration of what it means for the Christian to be in but not of the world.

Although there was always variety within religious camps, there were important differences between Protestant and Catholic approaches to the resacralization of life, and these were of great moment for the future of Europe and Christianity. Not surprisingly, Protestantism tended to resacralize life in an Augustinian way, while Catholicism, less so in France and more so in Spain or the Habsburg domains, followed Aquinas. At one pole stood Calvinist Geneva or Scotland, with their attacks on the very category of beauty, whether in theology or society. Here all that was not explicitly theological and edifying was suspect. At the other pole stood Italy or the Habsburg dominions, awash in beauty with a sensual profusion that sometimes escaped service to Christianity altogether. Here the ideal was the expression of the full range of human and divine reality, secular and sacred.

At the political level, in a manner analogous to Augustine's "theological imperialism", both Calvin's Geneva and, more cynically, the divine right theory of Elizabeth of England (r. 1558–1603), attempted to subject a whole citizenry to a form of theocracy in which the crown was not clearly subject to natural law categories. In Spain and the Habsburg dominions, by contrast, though there were partially parallel developments, the form of political life from the sixteenth century was quite different from that of the Protestant countries and, after the expulsions of the late fifteenth century, much more respectful of social variation and intermediary institutions. That is, granted a shared Christianity, the Spanish or Habsburg ideal was a federate monarchy composed of a great variety of regional and local entities, languages, and races. The one thing necessary was faithfulness to the texts of Ephesians and Hebrews already cited, that is, to the Reign of Christ.[13] But one faith, one baptism, did not necessarily involve one absolute monarchy, as in much of the north of Europe. Each level of society was to deal for itself with those

[13] Ayuso, "Francisco Elias de Tejada", 25, 30.

matters about which it reasonably could form expert information. The ideal was subsidiarity, to use a later word. The
function of the crown was to concern itself above all with
defense and foreign affairs: other matters could be dealt with
at their appropriate levels.[14]

Opinions about the nature and date of onset of modernity
are unending. For the most part Pierre Manent begins his
story of the rejection of the laws of God and nature with the
seventeenth century.[15] In important respects his argument is
not that different from that of Pope John Paul II, considered
in the next chapter; in declaring ourselves free, we have lost
our sense of what it is to be human. The distinguished medieval historian Peter Dinzelbacher goes back much further
and argues that we find the beginning of the modern deep
in the Middle Ages, in the period discussed in the last chapter, from 1050 to 1150.[16] At this time, he affirms, cultural
pluralism emerged, along with recognition of townsmen as a
part of society. A distinction between sacred and profane was
made, and intellectual life was rationalized. A sense of the
individual developed in attention to interior motivation and
conscience. Although Europe had always contained many
kinds of "cultural pluralism", one sees Dinzelbacher's point.
The development of urban life from deep in the Middle Ages
was both the cause and effect of increasing rationalization of
life, which expressed itself also in growing classifications of

[14] Glenn W. Olsen, "Unity, Plurality, and Subsidiarity in Twentieth-
Century Context", *Actas del III Congreso "Cultura Europea"* (Pamplona, Spain:
Thomson Aronzadi, 1996), 311–17.

[15] *The City of Man*, trans. Marc A. LePain, with a foreword by Jean Bethke
Elshtain (Princeton, N.J.: Princeton University Press, 1998).

[16] "Die 'Bernhardinische Epoche' als Achsenzeit der europäischen
Geschichte", in *Bernhard von Clairvaux und der Beginn der Moderne*, ed. Dieter
R. Bauer and Gotthard Fuchs (Innsbruck, Austria: Tyrolla-Verlag, 1996), 9–53.

all kinds, including distinction between the sacred and profane. Cities by their nature promote a variety of points of
view, and once their commercial functions are recognized as
legitimate, as they largely were by the time of Aquinas, they
in obvious ways set the course for the subsequent development of civilization. Seen in this perspective, the Baroque,
above all Baroque Rome, was a supremely successful attempt
to come to terms with the burgeoning urban and commercial life of the modern world. All that was different from the
rural life of the early Middle Ages was proudly displayed, but
in a public space configured and defined by great churches.
We might call this a modernity still under the reign of Christ.
We should, therefore, hesitate to see urban life as necessarily
generating attack on Christianity and seeking complete autonomy and the end of the reign of theology as queen.

The origins of this latter form of modernity, modernity as
quest for liberation from traditional authority, specifically from
Christianity, have been much debated. Catherine Pickstock,
in the manner of the historian of ideas, has pinpointed Duns
Scotus (d. 1308) as in his voluntarism, epistemology, and separation of ontology from theology the source of many of the
mistakes of this form of modernity.[17] She sees in Scotus an
especially important source of ideas that were to issue much
later in Enlightenment desire for control, objectivity, and
power. But perhaps we can usefully engage the question of
the origin of modernity as quest for autonomy by taking up
the somewhat eccentric views of the French thinker Marcel
Gauchet. In opposition to those who debate whether it was
Machiavelli or, later, Descartes (1595–1650) who was the pre-
cursor of modernity understood as rejection of Christianity,

[17] *After Writing: On the Liturgical Consummation of Philosophy* (Oxford: Blackwell Publishers, 1998).

Gauchet argues that Christianity had always carried within itself the seed of modernity.[18] Enlightenment thinkers of the eighteenth century who portrayed the Catholic Church as the enemy of reason and freedom, according to this analysis, merely expressed values Christianity had nurtured in them. As one reviewer has described the situation, "Voltaire's *Ecrasez l'infame* becomes, in Gauchet's story, the cry of a confused Christian."[19]

Beginning with the Incarnation and the sacrifice of Christ for the world's sins, Christianity gave a dignity to the world given by no other source. This far Gauchet seems right, but he then confuses the matter by suggesting that because Christ had entered human history, no subsequent Christian ruler could claim divinity. According to Gauchet, the fact that rulers could not claim divinity created a kind of space in which political liberty and the drive toward individual autonomy developed in Christian civilization. The individual did not exist simply to do the will of a divine ruler. Western rulers were mere men. Such an analysis needs much qualification. It ignores all the similarities and continuities great scholars such as Francis Dvornik pointed out between, for instance, *Early Christian and Byzantine Political Philosophy* and the pagan antecedents of the philosophy of those times.[20]

[18] I am using the analysis of Brian C. Anderson, "Modernity and Christianity Reconsidered", *First Things*, no. 84 (June/July 1998): 55–57 at 56. This is a review of Marcel Gauchet, *The Disenchantment of the World: A Political History of Religion*, trans. Oscar Burge, with a foreword by Charles Taylor (Princeton, N.J.: Princeton University Press, 1997). On Descartes see Marleen Rozemond, *Descartes's Dualism* (Cambridge, Mass.: Harvard University Press, 1998).

[19] Anderson, "Modernity and Christianity", 56.

[20] See his book *Early Christian and Byzantine Political Philosophy: Origins and Background*, 2 vols. (Washington, D.C.: Dumbarton Oaks Center for Byzantine Studies, 1966).

Theocracy understood not as rule by a divinity but as rule by a man whose will is to be obeyed because he is an agent of God is not simply some Oriental form of government, but has been a persistent Western institution, visible in the rules of Constantine, Justinian (r. 527–65), Charlemagne, and Otto I (r. 936–973), but also of Elizabeth I and Louis XIV (r. 1643–1715).

It was an argument of the preceding chapter that a theocracy endemic to Western civilization from the pharaohs to the French Revolution, which commonly had claimed that one was to be subject to the powers that be without reservation because they are God established, had been relatively pushed back by the Gregorian reform of the eleventh century. Whereas Charlemagne in the ninth century had claimed the divinely grounded right to direct the Church herself, both the eleventh-century Gregorian insistence that the God-given authority of secular rulers extended only to secular matters and a medieval tradition that saw possible grounds in either the natural or the eternal law for resisting the edicts of kings subsequently increasingly placed limits on the traditional claims of lay theocracy. Though rulers such as Frederick I Barbarossa or Philip IV, the Fair, of France (r. 1284–1314) frequently resisted these limits, they had some effect in the high and late Middle Ages, only to be undermined especially by Luther's idea that the good Christian should always obey the ruler, essentially a return to German theocracy.[21]

---

[21] William T. Cavanaugh, " 'A Fire Strong Enough to Consume the House': The Wars of Religion and the Rise of the State", *Modern Theology* 11 (1995): 397–420 at 399, gives a good explanation of how Luther's intention "to prevent the identification of any politics with the will of God" fed what I am calling theocracy: "In sanctifying that [coercive] power to the use of secular

This idea, Protestantism generally, was the return with a vengeance of the old categories of lay theocracy, now in the form of the *Landeskirche*, or state church. A ruler such as Elizabeth I of England might invoke divine right as a way of coping with very practical problems, rather than because she actually believed in it, but invoke it she did. Of course important shifts occurred over time, but the Catholic Louis XIV's Gallicanism controlled the Church in France more than Charlemagne's earlier theocracy ever had. Similarly, great Enlightenment enemies of the Church such as Joseph II of Austria placed the habits of theocracy in service of so-called enlightened absolutism. The state became God, as in some ways it has remained. With a logic explicable only by invoking his belief that everything should be in service to the state, Joseph simultaneously worked successfully to have Clement XIV suppress the Jesuits (1773) and he himself issued an Edict of Toleration (1781) in favor of the right to worship of Protestants and Jews. In the face of a powerless Pope (Pius VI), he issued "more than six thousand religious edicts, closed four hundred monasteries, forbade the kissing of relics and the clothing of statues, demanded warrants for pilgrimages, and reorganized seminaries".[22] Thus theocratic patterns of life, which extended deeply into both the pagan Germanic

---

government, . . . Luther contributed to the myth of the State as peacemaker which would be invoked to confine the Church. While apparently separating civil and ecclesiastical jurisdictions, the effect of Luther's arguments was in fact to deny any separate jurisdiction to the Church. Luther writes *To the Christian Nobility of the German Nation*, 'I say . . . that since the temporal power is ordained of God to punish the wicked and protect the good, it should be left free to perform its office in the whole body of Christendom without restriction. . . .' "

[22] The list was composed by Thomas F. X. Noble, "Popes for All Seasons", *First Things*, no. 86 (Oct. 1998): 34–41 at 39.

and Roman past, reasserted themselves especially in the Protestant divine right monarchies of the sixteenth and seventeenth centuries. These in turn transmogrified into the
enlightened absolutism, of whatever religious stripe, that, with
some irony, characterized the eighteenth century, the so-
called Century of Light, that closes our period. Here, though
the grounds of its authority had shifted, the state remained as
sacrosanct as ever it had been and exhibited a ruthlessness
against those who would not obey rarely found in the Middle Ages.

This said, though both Gauchet's facts and long-term perspectives are often astray, one can see his point. There is a
sense in which, as he says, Christianity, especially Latin Christianity, nurtures human autonomy. If *islam*, the idea that the
first thing asked of man is submission to God, is the first
requirement of Islam, the emphasis of Christianity is on the
cooperation of free creatures with their Creator. In comparison to Judaism or Islam, but also to Byzantium and Orthodoxy, Latin Christianity has usually found a place for the
secular, for various forms of qualified worldly autonomy.[23]
Whereas traditional Judaism and Islam have tried to base society solely on a book, on religious law, Europe ever since
Pope Gelasius I (492–96) has had a tendency, especially from
the side of the Church, to distinguish in some way between
two powers, temporal and religious, each with its own code
of law and proper responsibilities. This division arguably has
tended to foster the development of human autonomy. Ludwig Feuerbach (1804–1872) in the nineteenth century saw
this, though he thought it a good thing, while Gauchet does

[23] Shaul Bakhash, "Iran's Unlikely President", *The New York Review of Books*
[*NYRB*] 45, no. 17 (Nov. 5, 1998): 47–51, describes present-day Islamic criticism of the history of Islam in this regard.

not.[24] Gauchet holds that in our day Christianity in the Western world has resulted in a post-Christian society, in which men no longer need God because they have become fully autonomous.[25]

It does not seem to me, however, that one should conclude with Gauchet that this is the logical term of Christianity. If post-Christian autonomy embodies any Christian logic, it is more a logic implicit in Protestantism, particularly in the Protestant understanding of the principle of private judgment. Cardinal Newman made this connection in the nineteenth century. In their own ways a number of twentieth-century scholars seconded him. Thus George Marsden and James Burtchaell traced in a very convincing manner the steps by which especially Protestant schools became secularized, that is, autonomous from their founding religious traditions, in America.[26] So far as Catholicism is concerned, however, it seems to me that modernity as quest for complete autonomy is not a logical development of the Catholic tradition, but a perversion, an inability to stay within limits by continuing to affirm that a proper autonomy is always found in tandem with obedience to God.

Gauchet does not seem to me, therefore, to take the great early modernists seriously enough. Machiavelli understood himself not to be working out the logic of Christianity, but to be refusing it, and Thomas Hobbes' (1588–1679) goal was

[24] Anderson, "Modernity and Christianity", 56.

[25] Enrique Crespo, "Religión y Creatividad en Europa, Religion y Desarrollo Económico en Europa", *Actas del IV Congreso "Cultura Europea"* (Pamplona, Spain: Thomson Aranzadi, 1998), 313–23.

[26] George Marsden, *The Soul of the American University: From Protestant Establishment to Established Nonbelief* (New York: Oxford University Press, 1994); and James Burtchaell, *The Dying of the Light: The Disengagement of Colleges from Their Christian Churches* (Grand Rapids, Mich.: W. B. Eerdmans, 1998).

a *Leviathan* (1651), which had absorbed the Church and was free from the constraints of both nature and grace.[27] When in late eighteenth-century Paris a cult of reason attempted violently to eradicate religious institutions and de-Christianize society, this cult may instinctively have made reason itself into a religion, but that does not lessen the fact that the goal was freeing man entirely from Christian influence.[28] The main flaw in Gauchet's analysis, therefore, is his serious ignorance of the history of the idea of the Reign of Christ. Christianity of its nature instills not an unqualified autonomy but a qualified autonomy in which man is to realize himself through obedience to the truth. This is the point taught once again in the papal encyclical *Fides et Ratio* (1998).

Scholars continue to debate how we are to understand Saint Thomas More's *Utopia*, but this work, written in 1516, just as Luther was about to come to the attention of Europe, seems to me to have been very prescient in foreseeing the future of Christianity in a world torn between religious camps. However we are to understand *Utopia*'s treatment of religion, whatever the element of satire present, More seems to me to have been extraordinary in seeing what the dilemmas would be that Christianity would subsequently face. Recall that in this work of the imagination More portrays the Utopians as largely possessing a natural religion. They have had some minimal contact with Europe and have heard of Christianity, which has made some progress in Utopia, but the Utopians largely have the religion they had developed before

[27] Anderson, "Modernity and Christianity", 57. Joshua Mitchell, *Not by Reason Alone: Religion, History, and Identity in Early Modern Political Thought* (Chicago: University of Chicago Press, 1993), treats Luther, Hobbes, Locke, and Rousseau as political theologians employing a "politically authoritative history".

[28] Michel Vovelle, *The Revolution Against the Church: From Reason to the Supreme Being* (Columbus, Ohio: Ohio State University Press, 1991).

Christianity arrived. Interestingly—and this perhaps evidences the tendency of the humanists to reduce Christianity mainly to moral categories—Raphael Hythloday, the European traveller who has happened on Utopia, takes conversions to Christianity among the Utopians to have been helped by the fact that the Utopians understood Christianity to be very similar to the natural monotheism they already held.[29]

More portrays the traveller Raphael as interested not in the arts of war, but in those of peace, and the understood background of everything More says is More's own profound desire for peace in a Europe torn by dissension, much of it in some way nourished by religious division.[30] The main goal of the treatment of religion in *Utopia* is the delineation of the form religion must take if it is to lead to peace. Raphael says that he does not know whether the Utopians are right or wrong, but he does know that if one wants happiness, one must follow their principles.[31] Thus More the Christian humanist, in imagining Raphael's position into existence, already articulated the kind of "articles of peace" understanding of religion more familiar to Americans in the version developed for American history by John Courtney Murray.[32] Murray was in this respect More's heir.

---

[29] *Utopia*, 2nd ed., trans. and ed. Robert M. Adams (New York: W. W Norton, 1992), 73. Cf. the analysis of William C. Placher, *The Domestication of Transcendence: How Modern Thinking about God Went Wrong* (Louisville, Ky.: Westminister John Knox Press, 1996), which centers on the seventeenth-century construction of God to fit modernity. In Voltaire's (1694–1778) *Candide*, chap. 18, the inhabitants of Eldorado practice a natural monotheism.

[30] *Utopia*, trans. Adams, 8.

[31] *Utopia*, trans. Adams, 56–57.

[32] Cavanaugh, " 'A Fire Strong Enough to Consume the House' ", provides the proper setting in which to read Murray, but see specifically 410, 412. Cf. the analysis of John Milbank, *Theology and Social Theory: Beyond Secular Reason* (Oxford: Blackwell, 1993).

The logic of almost everything done in Utopia in regard to religion is that religion must be, as Erasmus (1466–1536) said, the cause of peace, not war. The Utopians' religious experiment is so important because by it they have obtained a large measure of peace.[33] Though they have Christians among them, the Utopians' religion pointedly is not Christianity, which, after all, brings the sword. The Utopians understand this, for their assumption is that if religion takes a supernatural form, men will always war and never agree. Indeed, while Raphael was in Utopia, one of the converts to Christianity caused trouble because of his zeal in preaching Christianity publicly. As soon as King Utopus had come to rule in Utopia, he had "decreed that every man might cultivate the religion of his choice, and might proselytize for it, provided he did so quietly, modestly, rationally, and without bitterness toward others".[34] Our hapless Christian had failed to meet these criteria. The thoughtful reader might note that, as in Pericles' praise of Athens in Thucydides' rendition of his funeral oration, or as in liberal ideology today, the toleration that is praised is a bounded toleration, closed to any who, in the words of the text, create "a public disorder".[35] Here More imagines into being the civil religion of later centuries.[36] *For the sake of peace*, religion is to be reduced to natural categories, what people *reasonably* can

[33] *Utopia*, trans. Adams, 41. I suppose it is part of the satire that the Utopians are allowed to fight to take underutilized land.

[34] *Utopia*, trans. Adams, 74, for this and the following phrase.

[35] On bounded toleration, see Glenn W. Olsen, "John Rawls and the Flight from Authority: The Quest for Equality as an Exercise in Primitivism", *Interpretation: A Journal of Political Philosophy* 21 (1994): 419–36, and "Religion, Politics, and America at the Millennium", *Faith and Reason* 22 (1996): 285–315.

[36] *Utopia*, trans. Adams, 78: in Utopia the priests are the censors of public morality (the enforcers of civil religion). The instruction they give children is of "great value in strengthening the state". Constantly religion is conceived as aiming at good citizenship. For orientation to discussion of civil religion, see

agree on. This is the thought experiment carried out by More in *Utopia*. Central is the idea that cultivation of natural reason tends to give as its fruits truth and unanimity, though it does not always achieve these.[37]

Much of the future of religion in the West was to be a quest, usually at the behest of the state, for some such "lowest common denominator" so that peace might be obtained. Without using the word *latitudinarianism* to describe the Utopians' approach to religion, Raphael notes in them an indifference to doctrine that is the natural consequence of conceiving religion as aimed at not disturbing public tranquility. Raphael tells us that "though there are various religions in Utopia ... they are like travelers going to one destination by different roads ... nothing is seen or heard in the churches that does not square with all the creeds. If any sect has a special rite of its own, that is celebrated in a private house ... in the churches no image of the gods is to be seen, so that each man may be free to form his own image of God after his heart's desire, in any shape he pleases ... their prayers are so phrased as to accommodate the beliefs of all the different sects." [38] In sum, the wish not to be or to be thought to be responsible for discontent and dissension in society has become central to the Utopians' notion of religion, and this inevitably has led to their not taking doctrine seriously, more generally to the privatization of religion. Here lay, if not the future of religion in the West, at least the future of any form of religion in service to the categories of good citizenship, peaceability, and not giving offense.

Glenn W. Olsen, "American Culture and Liberal Ideology in the Thought of Christopher Dawson", *Communio: International Catholic Review* 22 (1995): 702–20.

[37] *Utopia*, trans. Adams, 72–73.

[38] *Utopia*, trans. Adams, 79–80.

Christianity as one of the so-called high religions, that is, religions interested in truth, is in fact of its nature intolerant. On the spectrum of the world's religions, ranged between the poles of orthodoxy and orthopraxy, Christianity at the beginning and up to our period was as much interested in orthodoxy, correct belief, as it was in orthopraxy, correct practice. It is—that is until the sixteenth century it had always been—willing to struggle about matters of truth. From the viewpoint of later liberalism, its paradox had been that as a religion of peace it did bring the sword. Indeed, it conceived of love as carrying the obligation to bring others to the truth if possible, of course using only intrinsically just and Christian methods. More, it is important to note, not just here but elsewhere in his writings, with Erasmus, almost turned the traditional Christian understanding of peace on its head. For Augustine, since peace involves justice, bringing a society to peace might very well involve struggle and war. Peace was not the absence of war, but the presence of right order, and therefore customarily it was obtained at a price. Traditional Christian debate had centered on the question of how much justice or order in fact reasonably could be expected in this world, for it was understood that one would always have to pay the price for whatever peace was obtained. At some profound level More knew this very well, for his death paid the ultimate debt to truth. More's Utopians, by contrast, have not discovered Christian peace as traditionally understood, but rather the tranquility and cessation of fighting so much admired by Christian humanism in its sixteenth-century form, and then by many to the present.

The argument is that it is peace in this new, humanist, understanding that defines legitimate religion for the Utopians and is for many the way in which the relations between religion and society have been cast ever since. For it was just in

More's day that the nation-state was growing and theocracy was reasserting itself, complicating all discussion of religion. In the sixteenth-century, national-state form of theocracy, the universal Church was seen as an intruder in one's kingdom, a potential rival whose power had to be resisted. This also had been Charlemagne's and many medieval kings' view, but in a sixteenth-century context, the royal attack on the Church commonly took the form of portraying the Church as disruptive, as preventing internal "peace". This happened virtually everywhere, and Dante's (1265–1321) earlier running attack on the Papal States in both *De Monarchia* and *Commedia* shows how long such a point of view had been forming. Just as the Florentine Republican Dante refused to take responsibility for the fact that Italian unification was made impossible by the politics of Italy's great cities, above all his own, and instead laid the blame for disunity on the weakest of the Italian states, the Papal States, so from the sixteenth century, wars largely caused by the political ambitions of kings and nobles, by nationalism, were laid at the door of religion. This propaganda campaign on behalf of the state has been extraordinarily successful, and to the present most people of good will, for instance, accept labels such as "The Wars of Religion" as unproblematic.[39] Arguably those wars were much more caused by the state trying to create homogenous populations for itself than by religion.

The argument is that once peace in the humanists' sense was made the bottom line in discussion of religion, religion as traditionally understood was emasculated. A great deal of subsequent discussion of, for instance, Church-state relations was to be built on the premise that it is the Church that

---

[39] Cavanaugh, " 'A Fire Strong Enough to Consume the House' ".

must adjust to the needs of the state. Implicitly one's first loyalty belonged to one's state, rather than to the Church or to Christendom. What is good for the state is good. This of course was the view of More's contemporary Machiavelli: the Church was to leave the definition of the good to the state and was only tolerable if she herself was a good citizen and formed good citizens. One might note the irony of the views of this great opponent of Christianty eventually reappearing in, say, Modernism and Americanism. As to More himself, in *Utopia* he was merely constructing a work of the imagination, and again his martyrdom presumably shows that in fact he did not accept the logic of the nation-state. But I think he accurately saw what religion would have to become to be acceptable to the new political order aborning in his day.

In *Utopia* the state forces religious conformity only to the degree that it prohibits certain religious ideas it considers out of bounds; for the most part the hope is that the Utopians will one by one come to a right view of things if left to reason for themselves. This too foreshadows a logic of the future, again still alive in John Courtney Murray's thought. Common sense dictates that a people must have shared views. If these are not dictated by a monarch, if one will not allow them to be dictated by a monarch, the alternative of reason and democracy presents itself. Let each explore the issue and choose for himself. Obviously such an idea is close kin to the Protestant principle, thus perhaps the origin of More's notion that the natural religion of the Utopians is a rational religion in which by thought alone most have become monotheists. Such a view expresses great confidence in human nature and reasoning, and in this we espy a link between the humanists of the sixteenth century and the *Lumières* of the eighteenth. Both must lie about how good and how rational man is.

In the late sixteenth century and the first half of the seventeenth, the nations of Europe pressed their various causes, in which religion was inextricably involved, but, in one critical way, to no avail. No one was able to win Europe back to a single form of Christianity. The outcome was that increasingly it was realized that the most one could obtain by way of a shared, public religion was within the boundaries of a single principality or state. Already in 1555 the Peace of Augsburg had declared "his the region, his the religion", thus restoring traditional theocracy. Of course it took a long time after the Peace of Westphalia of 1648 for religion to become simply a private affair, for it was still very much a public matter within each of the European principalities. But the road marked out by the Utopians was now taken. Eventually classical liberalism would attempt to justify or rationalize the new situation, using arguments again well known to the Utopians. As noted earlier, the lesson liberalism thought it had learned was that there would always be war unless religion was kept out of the public sphere. Thus John Locke (1632–1704) proclaimed the linked ideas of toleration of various faiths, the separation of Church from state, and the primacy of the state over religion.[40] The nation-state was the real victor in the Wars of Religion. Now the modern state could demand exclusive loyalty. Or, as William Cavanaugh has argued, liberalism fostered the lie and—ironically, considering the fact that classical liberalism is supposed to wish to limit the state—did the state's work by insisting that the state was necessary to control religious passion: "The 'Wars of Religion' were not the events which necessitated the birth of the modern State: they were in fact themselves the birthpangs of

[40] See above, no. 27.

the state . . . to call these conflicts 'Wars of Religion' is an anachronism, for what was at issue in these wars was the very creation of religion as a set of privately held beliefs without direct political relevance."[41]

Among other things, the Catholic Baroque was a counter to all such attempts to privatize religion. It commonly carried with it the older idea that the Christian's first citizenship is in, if not explicitly the Church, at least Christendom, rather than the nation-state. Because it was articulated before the definitive breakdown of Christendom ratified by Westphalia in 1648, the Baroque was the last pan-European art form. It crossed confessional and class lines, but especially flourished in areas such as Italy or the Habsburg domains, in which, for whatever reason, the nation-state had not replaced older entities, whether princely, republican, federate, or imperial. As we have noted, the Baroque attempted to fill every public space it could to proclaim from the housetops the glory of God and the reign of Christ. But the Baroque did not simply find God in the world and proclaim his glory. In the wake of the Council of Trent (1545–63), it conveyed something of a program as to how the Catholic was to conduct himself in an early modern commercial and urban world, given to apostasy, divided in religion, and constantly threatened by the demand from secular rulers for obsequious loyalty.

This program had been articulated most clearly by Ignatius of Loyola (1491–1556) two generations before the first

[41] " 'A Fire Strong Enough to Consume the House' ", 398, also stating, "These wars were not simply a matter of conflict between 'Protestantism' and 'Catholicism', but were fought largely for the aggrandizement of the emerging State over the decaying remnants of the medieval ecclesial order." Of Locke Cavanaugh writes, p. 407, "Toleration is thus the tool through which the State divides and conquers the Church."

Baroque church was built in Rome. It aimed at supporting the Christian in a dangerous and hostile environment. Especially in the *Spiritual Exercises*, which he began to write in 1522, a year after Luther's excommunication, Ignatius found a way to form soldiers for Christ, people with steel wills who would not lose their bearing among all the conflicting attractions and temptations of early modern European culture. The idea was to develop a spirituality appropriate to an active life lived in the world, appropriate to finding God in all things and doing all for the greater glory of God. In comparison to the prayer of the medieval monk, which sought to free the mind from mental images and be still, Ignatius aimed at a form of meditation in which the mind was not stilled but seized images from the life of Christ to imitate and place one's life within that Life. Some have called this a theology of the laity or, on the other hand, of the Jesuit order, but Ignatius thought his *Exercises* appropriate to all who lived in the world, clergy or laity. The *Exercises* were written before he had founded the Jesuits, and he thought them suitable simply for the Christian as Christian. What Ignatius expressed in the *Exercises* was a new conception of the human imagination and of the power of imagining in relation to the making of decisions.[42] By meditation, by a life centering daily on the Eucharist and meditation, the Christian was to be formed to daily action within the world. At the moment that science was developing so rapidly, with its temptation to reduce reality to what could be quantified and providence to the categories of the laws of nature, the

---

[42] Antonio T. De Nicolas, *Ignatius de Loyola: Powers of Imaging: A Philosophical Hermeneutic of Imaging Through the Collected Works of Ignatius de Loyola, with a Translation of These Works* (Albany, N.Y.: State University of New York Press, 1986).

Ignatian stance articulated more clearly than ever before what the stakes are in living a human life.[43] Against the tendency toward disenchantment of the world, which was to grow ever more fully through the eighteenth century, Ignatius provided an alternative. Whereas the scientists increasingly viewed human creativity as centering on the mastery of nature, Ignatius' concern was the much more expansive Christian conception of man finding his place as cocreator with God.

For Ignatius the world was more a stage on which the drama of salvation was played out than a physical order that could be manipulated as soon as its regularity and laws were laid bare. Whereas the Calvinist response to the worldly tendencies of fourteenth- and fifteenth-century life had been to remove beauty from the world as a distraction to the religious soul, Ignatius, with the Baroque Catholicism that followed him, took another path. Here the glory of God was expressed first of all neither in civic nor domestic space, but in the liturgy, in an ecclesiological space that at once connected God and the soul through the altar. Liturgy is "the principal manifestation of God's worldly presence, ... the primordial place of God's glory".[44] That being so, the Christianization of public space discussed earlier was almost peripheral to Counter Reformation Catholicism in comparison to the articulation of the liturgy as the place in which the

---

[43] Steven Shapin, *The Scientific Revolution* (Chicago: University of Chicago Press, 1996), gives brief introduction to much current revisionism concerning the history of early modern science in relation to Christianity. See also Michael White, *Isaac Newton: The Last Sorcerer* (Reading, Mass.: Addison-Wesley, 1997). Alasdair MacIntyre, *After Virtue*, 2nd ed. (Notre Dame, Ind.: University of Notre Dame Press, 1984), esp. chap. 7, gives an excellent characterization of the competing views found in the late seventeenth and eighteenth centuries.

[44] M. Francis Mannion, "Liturgy and Beauty", *Antiphon* 3, no. 2 (1998): 2–3 at 3, said of the liturgy in general without reference to the sixteenth century.

interior development of the soul unites with the Church, where prayer meets ecclesiology. The idea was not to conform the liturgy to the world, but to conform the world to the liturgy. The world was to find its meaning through the liturgy. The goal of the Baroque era was no updating that simply brought the Church into conformity to the age, but a reform of the world that followed on the reform of the Church.

In a profound way Baroque art expressed a theology that sought to do justice to the vertical and horizontal orientations of human life. Simultaneously it witnessed to the glory of God and the greatness of man in a great meditation on the coming together of time and eternity in Christ. Both the horizontal and the vertical flow through him; he is that by which time and eternity are understood. Time is not, as Plato had it, simply a passing image of eternity; rather, eternity has entered time. Nowhere was this expressed more clearly than in the Baroque treatment of the Eucharist: generally in Baroque churches a shaft of light penetrates the church ceiling in order to fall on the altar, the earth-and-heaven-connecting center of reality, where time and eternity come together in a really present Christ. The liturgy dramatizes and celebrates the events of salvation history, opening into the eschaton and the coming of the Kingdom. In Rome itself the Swiss Guards, turned to the altar, fall on their knees and salute the Eucharistic Species at the Consecration.

The liturgy teaches that life in this world is not an end in itself; the significance of the world is found in the fact that it is a sign pointing beyond itself to the final goal of mankind, the consummation of time. Citing Alexander Schmemann to the effect that the liturgy realizes the Church by revealing her "as the epiphany of the Kingdom of God",

Avery Dulles has said that "liturgy serves to transform the old world into the new creation".[45] Arguably, so far as the Latin tradition is concerned, the Baroque saw more deeply than any earlier cultural expression, more than Romanesque or Gothic, the truth of this statement. The liturgy is eschatological in that it transforms our world into another, but this in a special sense. The liturgy realizes or makes present both the Church and the Kingdom of God. It makes the participant beautiful by making the Kingdom present or carrying him into a new order of things. Thus it is the most complete witness to the coming Lordship of Christ.[46] The *Catechism of the Catholic Church*, has declared, "The vocation of humanity is to show forth the image of God and to be transformed into the image of the Father's only Son" (no. 1877). In many ways the story we have been tracing, from Irenaeus' belief that the human face images God to the Baroque idea that the glory of God can be made visible in both marble and the life of the saint, is the story of this vocation of humanity to which the *Catechism* refers. If the seventeenth-century Catholic world had so many saints, this was in no small measure due to the coming together of Tridentine emphasis on attendance at daily Mass; Ignatian emphasis on an active life supported by the sacraments; and that most glorious of eschatological expressions, the Mass celebrated in a Baroque setting. This was the Catholic response to the disenchanted world of the Utopians.

---

[45] Avery Dulles, "Liturgy and Tradition: A Theologian's Perspective", *Antiphon* 3, no. 1 (1998): 4–20 at 6 and 9, citing Alexander Schmemann, *Liturgy and Tradition: Theological Reflections of Alexander Schmemann* (Crestwood, N.Y.: St. Vladimir's Seminary Press, 1990), 142.

[46] Schmemann, *Liturgy and Tradition*, 17.

Max Weber described Protestantism, specifically Calvinism, as having issued in the disenchantment of the world.[47] The foregoing has already suggested that, though in the long run there is much to be said for such a point of view, in the short run the story is more complicated. Still, from the first Protestantism disenchanted the world in some very specific ways, such as in teaching that the age of miracles was over. In Robertson Davies' *Fifth Business*, the Reverend Donald Phelps, Presbyterian minister of a small, early twentieth-century western Ontario village, advises the main character, a teenager who believes he has seen a miracle take place, in which his dead brother has been restored to life, "that it was blasphemous to think that anyone—even someone of impeachable character—could restore the dead to life. The age of miracles was past, said he, and I got the impression that he was heartily glad of it."[48] Later in the book a Jesuit and Bollandist, that is, a student of the saints, says to the main character, now an adult, "To be a Protestant is halfway to being an atheist . . . and your innumerable sects have not recognized any saints of their own since the Reformation, so called."[49] This Jesuit has the benefit of hindsight and sees the course that Protestantism and Europe have taken to the present. Still, if one lived about 1800, it could easily have seemed that a good deal of Europe was "halfway to atheism", certainly to disenchantment. The stark choice facing thoughtful men, which in the nineteenth century became

[47] John Patrick Diggins, *Max Weber: Politics and the Spirit of Tragedy* (New York: Basic Books, 1996), esp. chap. 4. There is a very illuminating defense of Weber's linking of "the Protestant ethic" to capitalist development in Robert Skidelsky, "The Mystery of Growth", *NYRB* 50, no. 4 (Mar. 13, 2003): 28–31.

[48] Middlesex 1970, 63.

[49] Ibid., 174. I thank my former colleague, Jeanne Ojala, for reading the present chapter and offering useful comment.

the choice between Enlightenment and Romanticism, already was present in the alternative of a world of disenchantment from which God has been removed, the world of Deism, Enlightenment, and much post-Newtonian science; or a Catholic and Baroque world in which God is found in all things and all is done to the glory of God, the world of Caravaggio (c. 1571–1610), Pedro Calderón de la Barca (1600–1681), and the brothers Asam (Cosmas Damian, 1686–1742; Egid Quirin, 1692–c. 1750).

V

The Church at the Turn
to the Third Millennium

In the last chapter I gave some consideration to the views of
the French thinker Marcel Gauchet, who believes that after
two thousand years, the Christian era stands at its end.[1] With
many others Gauchet thinks that the twenty-first century
will be a postreligious age, secular and centered on the values of "autonomy, democracy, science, and capitalism".[2]
Gauchet is far from the first person to say this. In the nineteenth century Ludwig Feuerbach (1804–1872) assailed Christianity, and Friedrich Nietzsche (1844–1900) proclaimed God
dead.[3] One may recall André Malraux's (1901–1976) dictum
that "the twenty-first century will be a religious century or
it will be nothing at all", but this does not make Gauchet
wrong. Gauchet's view is not that the churches will empty,

---

[1] Marcel Gauchet, *The Disenchantment of the World: A Political History of Religion*, trans. Oscar Burge, with a foreword by Charles Taylor (Princeton, N.J.:
Princeton University Press, 1997). There is an interesting exchange over the
nature of secularization or de-Christianization, and over how America and
Europe are to be compared, in *Church History* 71 (2002): 848–64.

[2] Thus the summary of Gauchet's views by Brian C. Anderson, "Modernity and Christianity Reconsidered", *First Things*, no. 84 (June/July 1998):
55–57 at 56.

[3] See Owen Chadwick, *The Secularization of the European Mind in the Nineteenth Century* (Cambridge, Eng.: Cambridge University Press, 1990), as at 49.

but that the religion found in those churches, in its relationship
to the past, "already inhabits a post-religious landscape".[4] To
the extent that the citizens of the democratic societies think
about such matters, their thought is largely given to accom-
modating whatever religion remains to the world outside the
churches. As Karl Barth observed of nineteenth-century Protestant theology, the world already sets the expectations to
which Christianity must conform.[5] Even if disillusioned and
no longer believing that the rapid changes of the contemporary era really mark human progress, such believers see no
alternative than simply to "hold on for the ride".

In response to such attitudes and views, toward the end of
the second millennium Pope John Paul II issued an apostolic
letter, *Tertio Millenio Adveniente*, on how Catholics were to
prepare themselves for the celebration of the arrival of the
third millennium and on how they were to live in that millennium.[6] This letter presented possibilities very different from
those offered by the tired liberalism Gauchet quite accurately describes.[7] The Pope's letter and the opportunities it
presents are the subject of the present chapter. In brief, I
wish to suggest that we now have enough distance on modernity to see at least many of its delusions or limitations and
to work for a postmodern world that, to stay for the mo-

[4] Anderson, "Modernity and Christianity Reconsidered", 57.

[5] Karl Barth, *Protestant Theology in the Nineteenth Century* (Grand Rapids,
Mich.: W. B. Eerdmans, 2002).

[6] The Pope dedicated each of the last three years of the millennium to one
of the Persons of the Trinity. In response three issues of *Communio: International Catholic Review* from 1997 to 1999 were dedicated to Son, Spirit, and
Father, the last to the Father, vol. 26 (1999): 235–357. John Paul II, *Agenda for
the Third Millennium*, trans. Alan Neame (London: HarperCollins, 1996), is a
collection of other relevant papal writings.

[7] Cf. my "Religion, Politics, and America at the Millennium", *Faith and
Reason* 22 (1996): 285–315.

ment with Gauchet's way of defining terms, is more post-secular than postreligious.[8]

My own view on such matters is in fact closer to that of Alan Ryan than it is to Gauchet. In the light of such developments as the growth of religious fundamentalism, often in close union with modernization, Ryan sees no reason to describe either the twentieth or some conceivable future century as simply secular.[9] Obviously much depends on how one defines terms. To keep things simple, we can define secularization in two quite different ways. First, secularization can denominate any process that leads to greater understanding of the *saeculum* (the temporal world or age), usually to the end of greater mastery of the world or "feeling at home" within it. Such secularization, say, the discovery of fire, has been going on a very long time and may mark a progress in human affairs. It was especially the subject of Chapter Three above. The second way of understanding secularization, as a tendency to disconnect the *saeculum* or world from God, treating some area or all of life as if God does not exist, is presumably what Gauchet and most people have in mind when they speak of secularization. If we call our age "secular" according to this usage, that simply means that the tendency to live as if God does not exist dominates our times.

[8] The distinction is Anderson's, "Modernity and Christianity Reconsidered", 57. For more nuance than I can provide in what follows on the possible ways of viewing and defining secularization and sacralization, see Glenn W. Olsen, "The Meaning of Christian Culture: An Historical View", *Catholicism and Secularization in America: Essays on Nature, Grace, and Culture*, ed. David L. Schindler (Notre Dame, Ind.: Our Sunday Visitor, 1990), 98–130, and "Cultural Dynamics: Secularization and Sacralization", *Christianity and Western Civilization*, ed. Wethersfield Institute (San Francisco: Ignatius Press, 1995), 97–122.

[9] "The Growth of a Global Culture", in *The Oxford History of the Twentieth Century*, ed. Michael Howard and William Roger Louis (New York: Oxford University Press, 1998), 63–76, and see no. 8 above.

The view I have been developing in previous chapters is that in fact in all known civilizations the sacred and the secular stand side by side, indeed often are intertwined. To speak of any civilization as simply secular or as simply sacred is to take some part of it for the whole. Typically in any period some aspects of life are becoming secular in one or the other meanings of that term, while others are being sacralized or resacralized, tied or retied to God. It is no more true that all forms of secularization are bad than that all forms of sacralization are good. Some of the religious fundamentalism Ryan describes illustrates this. Sometimes what starts as an arguably good form of secularization, say, Thucydides' (c. 460–c. 400 B.C.) attempt to see whether politics has its own laws, whether politics can be understood apart from reference to the gods by a methodological bracketing of the gods, ends up as a bad form of secularization, say, Machiavelli's (1469–1527) insistence that politics is all about power and not at all about providence. Machiavelli in effect made Thucydides' temporary methodological bracketing of the gods in order to study politics permanent. He declared God not to exist and ipso facto to have no possible bearing on the political or secular order.

There is every reason to believe that we will continue in the third millennium to experience simultaneously the attempt to live as if God does not exist and the attempt to resacralize life. As John Paul II declared in his encyclical letter *Veritatis Splendor*, 2, our task will be to sort all this out, to distinguish signs of hope from inappropriate forms of both secularization and sacralization: "The Church remains deeply conscious of her 'duty in every age of examining the signs of the times and interpreting them in the light of the Gospel, so that she can offer in a manner appropriate to each generation replies to the continual human questionings on the meaning of this life and the life to come and on how they are related.' "[10]

This chapter proposes to join the Pope in his examination of the signs of the times. Since the beginnings of the modern period, European culture has been engaged in a unique and fateful experiment, the disengagement of culture from religion, the formation of a culture that does not have religion at its center. All other historic cultures have, as Christopher Dawson observed, essentially been embodied religions.[11] The West has now been engaged for several centuries in the experiment of determining whether a culture can have any other basis. The pendulum swings from Renaissance to Reformation, or from Enlightenment to Romanticism, or now from Modernity to Postmodernity, while expressing an instinct to correct excesses, also arguably have expressed the intrinsic instability of a world without religion at its center.[12] The swings seem to become more violent as time passes,

[10] Trans. *The Splendor of Truth* (Boston: St. Paul Books and Media, 1993), no. 2, p. 11. The Pope is quoting *Gaudium et Spes*, 4, the Pastoral Constitution on the Church in the Modern World of the Second Vatican Ecumenical Council.

[11] For an introduction to Dawson's views, see my "The Maturity of Christian Culture: Some Reflections on the Views of Christopher Dawson", *The Dynamic Character of Christian Culture: Essays on Dawsonian Themes*, ed. Peter J. Cataldo (Lanham, Md., New York, and London: University Press of America, 1984), 97–125. I give them further attention in "The Changing Understanding of the Making of Europe from Christopher Dawson to Robert Bartlett", *Actas del V Congreso "Cultura Europea"* (Pamplona, Spain: Thomson Aranzadi, 2000), 203–10; and in another version in *Quidditas* 20 (1999): 159–70.

[12] "Postmodernism" can designate many not-always-compatible notions and is therefore susceptible to analysis from many points of view. The present essay concentrates on the possibilities Postmodernist critique of Modernity offers. Catherine Pickstock, *After Writing: On the Liturgical Consummation of Philosophy* (Oxford: Blackwell Publishers, 1998), is a deeply original attack on and response to Postmodernism of the form taken by Jacques Derrida. Both Postmodernism and Pickstock are considered by Aidan Nichols, "Hymns Ancient

and Eric Hobsbawm has rightly described the twentieth century as a time of extremes.[13]

A more theological and positive way of putting this would be to say that the dialectic of our culture—so far as I can see of all cultures—is such that its swings help articulate the full range of human possibility. Hans Urs von Balthasar illustrated this for the history of theology. Especially with late scholastic and early modern developments in mind, he remarked that while the history of theology may reveal a "waning of mental and synthetic powers", at the same time it has "brought what is distinctively Christian to more and more clarity".[14] Great questions about God, such as whether he changes or suffers or becomes sin (second Corinthians 5:21: "God made him [Christ] sin for us", Knox translation), have depths revealed only in the wake of "the apocalypse of the German soul", that is, the apotheosis of death in nineteenth- and twentieth-century German thought studied by von Balthasar in his doctoral thesis. Developments one may well lament often produce new insight.

In no case will the twenty-first century return to or restore some earlier age or historical situation. It will be either a world on the other side of liberalism and modernity or an alternative to liberalism and modernity, standing in their midst.[15] Immanuel Wallerstein has predicted that the first

and Postmodern: Catherine Pickstock's *After Writing*", *Communio* 26 (1999): 429–45, esp. 431–36.

[13] *The Age of Extremes: A History of the World, 1914–1991* (London: Pantheon Books, 1994).

[14] "Patristics, Scholastics, and Ourselves", in *Communio* 24 (1997): 347–96, at 385–86. Cf. the perspectives offered by Pickstock, *After Writing*.

[15] For one treatment of Modernity, see Marshall Berman, *All That Is Solid Melts into Air: The Experience of Modernity* (New York: Simon and Schuster, 1982).

quarter or half of the twenty-first century will be character-ized by the breakdown of the modern world system, by con-flict and disorder. Liberal ideology will be unable to retain its hegemony, and the nation-state system will dissolve.[16] In important ways, this contradicts Gauchet's vision of the fu-ture. Others predict different scenarios.[17] I am not a prophet and am very chary about such predictions. One can see ob-vious things, such as that Latin American immigration will continue to reshape the Church in America, or that Africa and Asia will have a large place in the Catholicism of the future, but even here it is very difficult to discern exactly what this means.[18] I simply wish to offer a reading of the prospects of the Church at the turn to her third millennium.

All the terms we need to use in our analysis—liberalism, modernity, postmodernity, and the like—are very slippery.[19] They are based in European history and do not apply equally to the whole world. Yet there are few places on the globe

[16] *Utopistics: Or, Historical Choices of the Twenty-First Century* (New York: W. W. Norton, 1998).

[17] For Christianity itself, see Robert Wuthnow, *Christianity in the Twenty-First Century: Reflections on the Challenges Ahead* (Oxford: Oxford University Press, 1993).

[18] On the swelling numbers of Latin American immigrants to the United States, see an article of Msgr. Lorenzo Albacete, *New York Times* (Feb. 28, 1999). For an account of the American Church at the end of the twentieth century, see Chester Gillis, *Roman Catholicism in America* (New York: Columbia University Press, 1999).

[19] I have had a good deal to say about the term "liberalism" and will not repeat myself here. In addition to nos. 7–8 above, see my "John Rawls and the Flight from Authority: The Quest for Equality as an Exercise in Primitivism", *Interpretation: A Journal of Political Philosophy* 21 (1994): 419–36; "Separating Church and State", *Faith and Reason* 20 (1994): 403–25; "American Culture and Liberal Ideology in the Thought of Christopher Dawson", *Communio* 22 (1995): 702–20; and "America as an Enlightenment Culture", *Actas del IV Congreso "Cultura Europea"* (Pamplona, Spain: Thomson Aranzadi, 1998), 121–28.

that have not been touched by the Western developments summarized by these terms, and reasons of economy force us to use them. "Modernism", or the modernist impulse of the late nineteenth and early twentieth century as a large social movement, especially exemplified in the arts, was built on a rejection of history and tradition in favor of abstraction and the creation of a new cultural space.[20] Commonly the idea was of an autonomous individual, free to create or express his own truth, and in this sense modernism continued an impulse epitomized by the French Revolution, the overthrow of traditional authorities.[21] Hence its relation to the broader phenomenon "modernity", associated especially with the Enlightenment and a certain understanding of reason, but also already with the Renaissance, and defined as a severing from the past which sets reason, science, and the individual free. Increasingly in such views, especially in recent decades and outside the so-called hard sciences, the idea of

[20] For general orientation, see Carl E. Schorske, *Thinking with History: Explorations in the Passage to Modernism* (Princeton, N.J.: Princeton University Press, 1998); Malcolm Bradbury and James McFarlane, eds., *Modernism: 1890–1930* (New York: Penguin, 1976); and Elizabeth Mankin Kornhauser and Amy Ellis, with Maura Lyons, *Stieglitz, O'Keeffe and American Modernism* (Hartford, Conn.: Wadsworth Atheneum, 1999). In literature Modernism could, minimally, designate the attempt to break free from literary conventions. In some fields, such as history, it can to the present designate what seems from the point of view of Postmodernism to be a fiction, the manner in which historians arrange their facts to create an argument: see the various books of Keith Jenkins, most recently *Why History? Ethics and Postmodernity* (New York: Routledge, 1999).

[21] Duncan McRoberts, "Tectonics and the Chapel of St. Ignatius at Seattle University", *Sacred Architecture* (Fall 1998): 16–17 at 16, articulates the issues so far as a religious use of Modernist architecture is concerned: "in Modernist architecture's preference for tectonic abstraction, there are no elements which can act as a symbolic link to the transubstantive and eschatological content of Catholicism.... As an abstraction, it becomes an architecture that forces the Catholic liturgy to occupy an otherwise empty, unknowable place."

objective truth has been in danger, stalked by the idea of a truth constructed by either society or the individual, that is, a truth not everywhere true but relative to social context. This was already a tendency in American pragmatism and is now found in many places, for instance, in the views about the history of science of Thomas S. Kuhn and of the public sphere of Jürgen Habermas.[22] Definitions vary, but this loss of confidence in reason as it has commonly been defined in the modern period often marks the passage from modernity to postmodernity, in the midst of which we find ourselves. However, as we will see toward the end of this chapter, post-modernity can be viewed more positively as discovery and critique of the arbitrary assumptions on which modernity was built, which had often been hidden from the view of just those who most thought themselves modern.

A question posed to twenty-first-century Christianity, so far as those parts of the world that have fallen under European influence are concerned, is the stance Christianity should take to modernity and postmodernity. The twentieth-century Church made three major efforts to respond to modernity, the third of which shaded into being also a response to postmodernity.[23] At the end of the nineteenth and into the early twentieth century, she responded to Catholic Modernism, which wished to adjust Catholicism to various new intellectual trends. Whatever one thinks of this episode or

[22] For both pragmatism and Habermas, see my "The Quest for a Public Philosophy in Twentieth Century American Political Thought", *Communio* 27 (2000): 340–62; Thomas Kuhn, *The Structure of Scientific Revolutions*, 3rd ed. (Chicago: University of Chicago Press, 1996); and Thomas Nickles, ed., *Thomas Kuhn* (New York: Cambridge University Press, 2003).

[23] I am both using and adjusting the analysis of Russell Shaw, "Responding to the Crisis of the Church", *New Oxford Review* 66, no. 3 (Mar. 1999): 8–13 at 9.

series of episodes, one could argue that it showed the need
for a more Socratic method of response on the part of the
Church and papacy to the modern age than she then exer-
cised.[24] That is, the Church, as earlier in the case of the
Syllabus of Errors (1864), was more successful in isolating
what was wrong in the views of the Modernists than in
placing what was right in their views in a more adequate
framework than the Modernists themselves had been able to
achieve.[25]

Arguably, the second major twentieth-century ecclesiastical effort to respond to modernity, the Second Vatican Council, was more sophisticated in such matters, but again only a
partial success, sometimes, at least in implementation, naive
and overly optimistic. Most successful in responding to modernity and postmodernity was the third major effort of the
twentieth-century Church, the pontificate of John Paul II
itself. Many Popes had challenged various aspects of modernity, but John Paul was the first to confront the whole
twentieth-century development, including the shading of modernity into postmodernity. If modernity generally expressed great confidence in a certain Cartesian and Newtonian
concept of reason, postmodernity was sometimes defined by

[24] Thomas F. X. Noble, "Popes for All Seasons", *First Things*, no. 86 (Oct.
1998): 34–41 at 40, gives the Popes rather high marks for their guidance of the
Church through the Modernist controversy: "whereas biblical scholarship split
Protestantism into factions, some of which turned the Bible into just one good
book among many while others became 'Fundamentalist,' Catholic thinkers
were encouraged by *Providentissimus Deus* (1893) and then by *Divino Afflante
Spiritu* (1943) to apply to the text of Holy Writ all the tools of modern science."

[25] Another way of putting this is that the criticism of liberalism begun by
Pius IX remains incomplete: see my "Religion, Politics, and America at the
Millennium", and Peter Toon, "Christianity and Subjective Human Rights",
Touchstone 11, no. 6 (Nov./Dec. 1998): 31–35. See also the defense of Pius IX
and Pius X by Noble, "Popes for All Seasons", 36, 39, and 41.

a loss of confidence in reason in any form. Especially in his thirteenth encyclical, *Fides et Ratio*, issued in 1998, John Paul proffered a fuller concept of reason than was common in modernity's reduction of reason to its quantitative, scientific, and utilitarian dimensions, and he defended this concept against the despair of some forms of postmodernity.

At the turn to the twenty-first century, three options presented themselves to Catholics trying to work out a response to their historical situation.[26] First they could, in the manner of either sectarianism or certain forms of integralism, reject all accommodation to the world. However, this seemed inadmissable to those who took the catholic and incarnational dimensions of Catholicism seriously, for in some mysterious way the goal of Catholicism is that the Church herself become *forma mundi*.[27] The second option, accommodation of the Church to the world, was much more common, but its limitations were becoming every day clearer. Thus, in words originally published in French in 1973, Leszek Kolakowski delineated the Christian dilemma as it stood in the wake of Vatican II:[28]

> Fearful lest it become relegated to the position of an isolated sect, Christianity seems to be making frenzied efforts at mimicry in order to escape being devoured by its enemies—a reaction that seems defensive, but is in fact self-destructive. In the hope of saving itself, it seems to be assuming the colors of its environment, but the result is that it loses its identity,

[26] Again I am using and reflecting on the propositions put forward by Shaw, "Crisis of the Church", 9 and 13.

[27] John Paul II, "Talk in Argentina", *Origins* 12 (June 24, 1982): 87–89 at 89, used the term *forma mundi* to describe how the Church is related to the world.

[28] *Modernity on Endless Trial* (Chicago: University of Chicago Press, 1990), 69.

which depends on just that distinction between the sacred and the profane, and on the conflict that can and often must exist between them.

Some may disapprovingly think of accommodationism as a mistaken path taken by the Vatican Council's opening of "a window to the world", but it was in fact much older, in some ways as old as faith itself. We have noted that as long as the nation-state had been developing, that is, for centuries, the state had demanded loyalty of its Christians and frequently had forced the Church to conform to its desires.[29] Nationalism had almost always involved a retailoring of Catholicism to politically determined national needs. In an American context most Catholics, like most Americans, had in fact freely chosen the assimilationist or accomodationist path, wishing above all to be considered good Americans and to succeed. Over time they seemed more and more American and less and less Catholic. This second option of accommodationism was often a form of easing one's conscience and at least largely losing one's religious identity in pursuit of worldly success. It is now a commonplace that the churches that have most thoroughly followed this option, the most adaptive churches, have lost their membership.[30]

---

[29] William T. Cavanaugh, " 'A Fire Strong Enough to Consume the House': The Wars of Religion and the Rise of the State", *Modern Theology* 11 (1995): 397–420.

[30] In *The Churching of America, 1776–1990: Winners and Losers in Our Religious Economy* (New Brunswick, N.J.: Rutgers University Press, 1992), Rodney Stark and Roger Finke developed the argument, in the words of a review by Elizabeth A. Clark in *The American Historical Review* 103 (1998): 153–54 at 153, "that religious movements demanding adherence to strict doctrine and practice grow, while groups modernizing their doctrine and embracing the values of wider society decline. This is a claim that runs counter to the prevailing secularization hypothesis."

The third option, that advocated by John Paul, being "in but not of the world", was also as old as Christianity. Superficially it could be viewed as a mixture of the other two options, for it recommended a prudence or discernment that sometimes rejected and sometimes accepted worldly developments. But it has its own integrity and is better understood as an evangelical openness to culture aimed at culture's conversion, which is to preserve and develop what is already good while purifying what is evil. When at the turn to the third millennium the Pope wrote of a "springtime for Christianity", this seems to be what he had in mind.[31] The twenty-first century was to be a time of evangelization in which goods already present were to be teased out, but by a process that the Pope presumed would be painful, since it in part involved describing as evil or imperfect things that many called good.

Tertio Millenio Adveniente expressed ideas that had been long developing in John Paul's mind. As Cardinal Wojtyla in 1976, he gave the papal Lenten retreat, choosing the theme "Sign of Contradiction".[32] The idea that the Church and Christians are to be signs of contradiction was thereafter central to John Paul's thinking about the third millennium. In this the materialism and secularism of modern life were the prime targets of his critique of modernity. He understood the former as a use of the goods of the world without regard to God, an attachment to property as a good in itself not in service to other goods. Secularism was similarly the living of life without reference to God, hermetically within the confines of the age and captive to the age's values. John Paul's

---

[31] This is the message of *Redemptio Missio*, in which John Paul II was speaking specifically of the Church in Africa and Asia.

[32] Karol Wojtyla, *Sign of Contradiction* (New York: Seabury Press, 1979).

attack was on neither wealth nor secularity per se, for the former, properly used, may hasten the Kingdom of God, and the latter may advance a proper human domination of life that alleviates suffering and builds up knowledge.

When Cardinal Wojtyla became John Paul II, he meditated on the significance of the existence of his pontificate between Vatican II and the advent of the millennium. Cardinal Avery Dulles has correctly observed that the advent of the millennium "may be seen as a hermeneutical key for his entire conduct of the papacy".[33] The notion of inculturation of the Gospel was central to John Paul's view. In Dulles' summary:[34]

> In the pope's vision, the gospel cannot take hold of individual persons and societies except by being incarnated, so to speak, in cultures. Western European culture, in spite of its past greatness, no longer suffices for a world Church. Every cultural sector, including those of Asia and Africa, has a proper contribution to make in showing forth the full riches of Christ the redeemer. By implanting itself in various cultures, the gospel preserves, elevates, and purifies those cultures, supplementing whatever may be lacking in them ... the Church hears a call to evangelize not only individuals but cultures themselves. In so doing, the Church and its representatives must not fear to become signs of contradiction.

Signs of contradiction exist both for themselves, as witnesses to the truth, and as prods to a fruitful inculturation of the gospel. Examination of conscience must precede this incul-

---

[33] Avery Dulles, "John Paul II Theologian", *Communio* 24 (1997): 713–27 at 719. In "Orthodoxy and Social Change", *America* (June 20, 1998), Dulles argued that orthodoxy must be "countercultural, at least in the sphere of religion".

[34] Dulles, "John Paul II Theologian", 725–26.

turation, for the Church in the long course of her history has been not simply the source of great benefits to mankind. Christians have made mistakes and done much evil, hence the Pope's call to repentance on the eve of the millennium as a preparation for the purification of human culture. "If Christians are to walk upright in the next millennium, they must cross the threshold of the year 2000 on their knees." [35]

In an *Ad Limina* address to the Australian bishops, John Paul elaborated on the desired relation between Church and world: [36]

> The advanced secularization of society brings with it a tendency to blur the boundaries between the Church and the world. Certain aspects of the prevailing culture are allowed to condition the Christian community in ways which the Gospel does not permit. There is sometimes an unwillingness to challenge cultural assumptions as the Gospel demands.... This attitude embodies a too optimistic view of modernity, together with an uneasiness about the Cross and its implications for Christian living.... All this causes uncertainty about the distinctive contribution which the Church is called to make in the world.

What the Church provides the world, according to John Paul, is what Pope Paul VI called a *colloquium salutis*, a conversation about true human flourishing. [37] This is not a one-way monologue in which some previously non-Christian culture

---

[35] Richard John Neuhaus, "Forgive Us Our Trespasses", *First Things*, no. 87 (Nov. 1998): 74–75 at 75, summarizing the Pope's thought in *Tertio Millennio Adveniente*.

[36] John Paul II, "*Ad Limina* Address to Australian Bishops", *Adoremus Bulletin* 4, no. 9 (Feb. 1999): 6–8 at 6.

[37] John Paul II, "*Ad Limina* Address to Australian Bishops", 6. For very specific examples of inculturation, see Lamin Sanneh, *Translating the Message: The Missionary Impact on Culture* (Maryknoll, N.Y.: Orbis Books, 1989).

receives the gospel, but a true conversation in which the Church herself comes to realize her own nature more fully through dialogue with the cultures.[38] Thus, as in the ancient period the Church came better to understand and express herself by dialogue with the categories of Greek culture, Hans Urs von Balthasar has suggested that at least on some questions an even greater conversation lies before the Church in her encounter with Buddhism.[39] This should be one of the great dialogues of the third millennium.

The categories of martyrdom and paschal sacrifice were never far from John Paul II's mind. The idea was that the Church and the Christian must both love the world and wish to dialogue with it, but also because of love of the truth be willing to challenge cultural assumptions and live in a countercultural and persecuted way. The great danger was assimilationism, losing one's identity, being so afraid of being isolated from the larger culture that one becomes that culture. Likely the price to be paid for continuing the traditional Christian labors of being within but not of the world,

---

[38] Cardinal Joseph Ratzinger has given special attention to inculturation, dialogue, and the self-transcendence of cultures. He sees all cultures as, in their search for God, called to transcend themselves. In an article composed by an anonymous editor from excerpts of an address given by Ratzinger on Feb. 13, 1999, "Culture and Truth: Reflections on *Fides et Ratio*", *Adoremus Bulletin* 5, no. 2 (Apr. 1999): 1, 4 at 4, Ratzinger states, "The encounter [of Christianity with Greek culture] was made possible because . . . a . . . process of transcending the particular had begun in the Greek world. The fathers of the Church did not simply mix an autonomous and self-standing Greek culture into the Gospel. They were able to take up the dialogue with Greek philosophy and use it as an instrument for the Gospel, because in the Greek world a form of autocriticism of their own culture—which had already arisen through the search for God—was already under way."

[39] See for instance "Philosophy, Christianity, Monasticism", in *Explorations in Theology*, vol. 2: *Spouse of the Word* (San Francisco: Ignatius Press, 1991), 333–72.

of participating in secular culture while maintaining a certain distance from it, and of inculturating the faith would be very high, but the price of cowardice in the confrontation of these tasks would be even higher.

The theme of *Tertio Millennio Adveniente* came from Hebrews 13:8, "Jesus Christ is the same today as he was yesterday and as he will be for ever" (Jerusalem version). This is the ultimate ground of Christian confidence in the twenty-first century. The French Canadian theologian Cardinal Marc Ouellet has written a typically profound meditation on the implications of this verse. He, with the Pope and many others, argues that the counterculturalism called for in the twenty-first century must be communal as well as individual.[40] The oppressiveness of the culture in which we live tends to isolate people who resist it either individually or in some form of sectarianism. The Catholic Church cannot be content with either of these. Because Catholicism is a trinitarian religion that affirms that at the center of being is loving relation between persons ("God is Love"), its goal must be the creation of *communio* in a form suitable to the times.

Before we consider Ouellet's and others' proposals as to what the Catholic future might be, there is a more basic consideration. In many ways the most acute Catholic political observers of our times—I think of the Anglo and Roman Catholic theologians at Cambridge University associated with the movement called "Radical Orthodoxy"—recover some form of Augustine's idea of the City of God as *altera civitas*, "the other city".[41] The motives here doubtless are various.

---

[40] "Jesus Christ, the One Savior of the World, Yesterday, Today, and Forever", *Communio* 24 (1997): 221–33 at 223–24, on this and the following.

[41] Donald X. Burt, *Friendship and Society: An Introduction to Augustine's Practical Philosophy* (Grand Rapids, Mich: W. B. Eerdmans, 1999), gives orientation

Some may suspect that whatever "establishment" Christianity has had in the past is over and that most political orders must be viewed as at least in some degree hostile to Christianity. Some may greet various signs of Christian vitality and influence on the larger culture and still believe that in the long run the primary Christian responsibility is for the state of the Church, not for the fate of whatever political order a church finds itself within. Some may believe—and this actually was Augustine's belief too—that though the Christian's first citizenship is in the Church, he is obligated also to work for the Christianization of the times.[42] In the United States, some may look back to the period of European immigration, a time when the Catholic Church in America constructed a state within the state, an interconnected series of institutions embracing all aspects of a Catholic's life, and they wish for something at least vaguely similar in our own day.[43]

Ancient Christians, even before Augustine, when asked where their citizenship lay, sometimes responded that they belonged to "another city", that is, a "city" other than the Roman Empire. In the second century, the Epistle to

---

to Augustine's ecclesiological and political thought. See also Carol Harrison, *Augustine: Christian Truth and Fractured Humanity* (Oxford: Oxford University Press, 2000), 62 and Part II.

[42] Thus I disagree with Robert A. Markus' analysis of Augustine as found in *Saeculum: History and Society in the Theology of St. Augustine*, rev. ed. (Cambridge, Eng.: Cambridge University Press, 1970), and *Gregory the Great and His World* (Cambridge, Eng.: Cambridge University Press, 1997). It seems to me that the notion of the secular (*saeculum*) Markus attributes to Augustine, namely an intermediate, religiously neutral, realm between the sacred and the profane, is not something actually in Augustine, but a reading into his thought of the liberal idea that there could, and ought, be such a realm.

[43] Mary Ann Glendon, "The Hour of the Laity", *First Things*, no. 127 (Nov. 2002): 23–29 at 24–27.

Diognetus had already spoken of Christians as being like transients in their countries. Though they took their part as citizens, they were aliens and their homeland a foreign country. This is the view Augustine inherited. While citizens of Rome, Christians' ultimate citizenship lay elsewhere. They were citizens of "another country", not yet clearly visible but forming in time. This is the stance that Radical Orthodoxy urges as appropriate to our times. Strongly dissenting from all those liberal and accommodationist views that privilege the modern nation-state as the assumed context that defines and should define modern life, theologians such as John Milbank use Augustine's view of the City of God to develop an ecclesiology in which the historical, institutional Church becomes the locus of all Christian life, including political life.[44] The idea here, found also in the work of such theologians as Stanley Hauerwas and Michael Baxter, is that the Christian's first citizenship is in the Church.[45] The Christian recognizes the

---

[44] John Milbank, *Theology and Social Theory: Beyond Secular Reason* (Oxford: Blackwell, 1993). Ashley Woodiwiss, "Revising Our Pledges of Allegiance", *Touchstone* 11, no. 5 (Sept./Oct. 1998): 28–33 at 30–31, while giving a good account of these theologians, used in what follows, slides from the language of *altera civitas* to that of "Church". Augustine did not customarily equate either of his Two Cities, both of which are invisible and defined by a type of love, to some earthly entity. The City of God was not the Church, and the City of Man was not the empire. See on this Étienne Gilson, "Foreword", to *Saint Augustine: The City of God*, trans. Gerald G. Walsh, Demetrius B. Zema, Grace Monahan, and Daniel J. Honan, ed. Vernon J. Bourke (Garden City, N.Y.: Doubleday, 1958), 13–35 at 26–29, and Yves M.-J. Congar, "'Civitas Dei' et 'Ecclesia' chez saint Augustin. Histoire de la recherche, son état présent", *Revue des Etudes Augustiniennes* 3 (1957): 1–14, noting also that though for Augustine the Church is visibly expressed in the *communio sacramentorum*, it is in its highest reality a *societas sanctorum* whose boundaries cannot be delimited within history.

[45] See "The Kingship of Christ: Why Freedom of 'Belief' Is Not Enough", by Stanley Hauerwas with Michael Baxter in Hauerwas' *In Good Company:*

kingship of Christ, not necessarily in the form of the confessional state but as meaning that all politics must be grounded
on the fact that Christ is King. The Church as *altera civitas* in
Augustine's sense aims at peace rather than dominance, that
is, upsets worldly values, and by the very fact that it is Christian is the matrix of a countercultural life.[46] Especially the
Catholic essentially accepts Rousseau's criticism that the Catholic has "two legislative orders, two rulers, two homelands,
and . . . [there might be a quibble here as to the necessity of
the contradiction] two contradictory obligations".[47]

   Christ found the Kingdom of God not necessarily in families according to blood but among those "brothers" and "sis-
ters" who did the will of God and thus formed a new kind
of spiritual family.[48] Augustine similarly declared that true
families are those where peace and love are present. In this
spirit, the proposal is that for the Christian the primary "polity" is neither family nor nation-state, but the Church. This
is a Church that contains singles and the homeless, worships
in a liturgy that helps all behold the glory of God, and is

The Church as Polis (Notre Dame, Ind.: University of Notre Dame Press, 1995),
199–216 at 215: "we write not as apologists for the liberal project . . . nor as
theorists groping for a way to make peace with the nation-state, but as theologians of a church constituted by a politics that acknowledges Christ as King. . . .
Finally, we are aware that some will infer from what we have written that we
favor some kind of restoration of 'the confessional state'. We favor no such
restoration. However, we do favor restoring a theoretical commitment to
grounding politics in the christological claim that Christ is King."

[46] Jacques Derrida confronts various aspects of Radical Orthodoxy in ex-
changes in *Questioning God*, ed. John D. Caputo, Mark Dooley, and Michael J.
Scanlon (Bloomington, Ind.: Indiana University Press, 2001).

[47] Quoted in Peter C. Meilaender, "Christians as Patriots", *First Things*,
no. 130 (Feb. 2003): 31–35 at 32.

[48] Francis Martin, "Marriage in the New Testament Period", in *Christian
Marriage: A Historical Study*, ed. Glenn W. Olsen (New York: Herder and Herder,
2001), 50–100 at 58–61, 65–69.

incarnated in a textured, local existence.[49] "All 'political theory', in the antique sense, is relocated by Christianity as thought about the Church."[50] The family in an obvious sense remains the first human community, but the Church, rather than the state, should provide us our basic orientation to life shared in society. It is not that the Church takes some specific political line or usurps tasks for which she has no special competence or loses her liturgical and contemplative center. It is rather that in her everyday embodiedness or institutional character the Church leads us to ask such specific questions as whether parochial schools, or perhaps home schools, are not more appropriate to membership in that *altera civitas* than the schools of the state, with all their indoctrinaton toward "good citizenship".[51]

The goal is a cycle of everyday existence formed around life in the Church, both universal and local. Whatever the limitations of pre–Vatican II Catholic life, it provided a comprehensive form of existence including everything from frequent confession to a rich liturgical life to the activities of the Knights of Columbus. Since the Council—and this is the work of many factors, but especially of the tendency of a media-driven culture to present reality not holistically but as a series of sound bytes—this has been largely lost, in fair

[49] Woodiwiss, "Revising Our Pledges of Allegiance", 32, using Rodney Clapp, *Families at the Crossroads* (Downers Grove, Ill.: InterVarsity Press, 1993): see esp. chaps. 4–5.

[50] Milbank, *Theology and Social Theory*, 406, cited by Woodiwiss, "Revising Our Pledges of Allegiance", 33. Cf. Michael J. Baxter, "From Weber to Aristotle and Beyond: The Journey of a Catholic Sociologist", *The Catholic Social Science Review* 3 (1998): 9–27 at 24–27.

[51] Woodiwiss, "Revising Our Pledges of Allegiance", 33, citing John H. Westerhoff, "Fashioning Christians in Our Day", in *Schooling Christians: "Holy Experiments" in American Education*, ed. Stanley Hauerwas and John H. Westerhoff (Grand Rapids, Mich.: W. B. Eerdmans, 1992), 262–81 at 266.

degree consciously destroyed by influential clergy. Thus, as R. Scott Appleby observed in an address to the Catholic Academy for Communication Arts Professionals:[52]

> The challenge of Catholic education and formation in our media-driven, cyberspace age is no less than this: older Catholics must be restored to and younger Catholics introduced to a sense of Catholicism as a comprehensive way of life—as a comprehending wisdom and set of practices that bring integrity and holiness to individuals and to the families and extended communities to which they belong and which they serve.

This life must center around the Church's calendar more than around the secular calendar, around the saint of the day more than around Independence Day. One hopes that the bishops, many of whom seem locked into a mentality that considers continuing secularization inevitable, will aid this process by stopping their concessions to secular culture in the matter of "reducing and obfuscating the nature of traditional Catholic holy days".[53] For some, caught in terrible parish situations,

---

[52] *Origins*, Nov. 7, 2002, quoted in Richard John Neuhaus, "While We're at It", *First Things*, no. 130 (Feb. 2003): 74–84 at 77 and 81.

[53] Owen F. Cummings, "How Adequate Are the Postconciliar Catholic Funeral Rites", *Antiphon: Publication of the Society for Catholic Liturgy* 3, no. 3 (1998): 15–32 at 21. There clearly are bishops who understand the issues. The "NCCB Report", *Adoremus Bulletin* 4, no. 8 (Dec. 1998–Jan. 1999): 1–8 at 5, reports a debate at the semiannual meeting of the National Conference of Catholic Bishops in Washington, D.C., Nov. 16–19, 1998, about moving Ascension Thursday to Sunday. Bishop Alfred Hughes of Baton Rouge is quoted as saying "[m]y continuing concern is accommodation to our culture, and the backing away from sacrifice, and the loss of a sense of transcendence. And these are issues that are recurring, and every time we take a step in the direction that's being proposed, it seems to me that we yield a little bit more about our identity in the culture that we want to transform as well as find ourselves incultured into." Bishop Raymond Burke of LaCrosse said, "[W]e are making

none of this will work. But thinking along these lines reminds us that twenty-first-century Christians, likely living in a cultural context hostile to Christianity, will in some way have to begin their thought at home or locally, with some everyday instauration of Christian life. As Romano Guardini wrote in the years following World War II, Christian life in the future will likely be characterized by danger at every step and opposition from the larger culture. In one way or another, Christians will have to fall back on other witnessing Christians.[54]

Frederick Bauerschmidt, in noting that the gospel has its own proper cultural form, namely, the life of the Church herself, has come to a conclusion complementary to that of Radical Orthodoxy.[55] Though the Church has played a significant role in the formation of many cultures, she is not, Bauerschmidt observes, to be equated with any of these. That is, though there has been, for instance, an especially close tie between the Church and Western culture, and there is nothing wrong in a Christian worrying about the fate of the culture thus formed, undue attention to this fate may obscure the fact that Christianity sits somewhat loosely in relation to all cultures in which it finds itself, except for one.[56] This last is the Church herself, which is something

---

the transfer in order to make it more convenient for people to observe the solemnity at the price of losing the sense of sacred time, and the sacrifice which we need to make in order to observe sacred times."

[54] *The End of the Modern World: A Search for Orientation*, trans. Joseph Theman and Herbert Burke, ed. with an introduction by Frederick D. Wilhelmsen (New York: Sheed and Ward, 1956).

[55] The following depends on the description of Bauerschmidt's thought by Lauren Pristas, "The 1998 SCL Chicago Conference", *Antiphon* 3, no. 3 (1998): 44–46 at 44.

[56] *The Future of the European Past*, ed. with an introduction by Hilton Kramer and Roger Kimball (Chicago: I. R. Dee, 1997), presents some scenarios.

like a culture.[57] Especially in the lives of the saints and in art, architecture, music, and literature, the history of the Church carries the history of Christian imagination. The Church too has a comprehensive worldview, expressed by her contemplatives and theologians and embodied nowhere more fully than in the liturgy, which is to provide the Christian's basic orientation toward life. All these things, but first the liturgy, make the Church a culture with a distinctive identity. This is a culture at once universal and particular, but because we are embodied beings, we normally share in this culture through some specific parish and liturgy. Once again, the conclusion that follows is that it is the culture of the Church herself to which the Christian owes his first allegiance and from which he should obtain his orientation to the larger world. As John Paul II expressed it on May 30, 1998, "Catholic identity . . . comes from . . . living within the Church today and always, speaking from the heart of the Church to the contemporary world." [58]

The views of the theologians of Radical Orthodoxy or of Bauerschmidt did not spring full grown from the ground. They had important precedents earlier in the twentieth century. One recalls particularly Virgil Michel's (1890–1938) vision of the organic unity between liturgy and social action,

---

[57] Cf. David Mills, "Wilken on Engaging the Culture", *Touchstone* 11, no. 6 (Nov./Dec. 1998): 6–7 at 6: "As Robert Wilken said in *Christian History*, the early Church began by demanding of people a new way of life. . . . It built 'its own sense of community, and it let these communities be the leaven that would gradually transform culture'. The church 'was not something that spoke to its culture; it was itself a culture and created a new Christian culture'."

[58] "Address of the Pope to the Bishops of the United States", *Fellowship of Catholic Scholars Quarterly* 21, no. 4 (Fall 1998): 37–39 at 39. The Pope was speaking in regard to Catholic universities, but his words apply equally well to the Church herself.

which had important similarities to the thought and practice of Dorothy Day (1897–1980). As Keith F. Pecklers described Michel's vision:[59]

> Michel believed that the contemporary Church was called to take on the form and shape of the mystical Body, paradigmatically expressed in the Eucharist. Since the Mystical Body was not merely a supernatural reality but a model for a renewed human society, the retrieval of this theme as a fundamental eucharistic spirituality challenged Christians to view themselves not merely as organically linked to Christ, but to all who shared life in that same body.

A great irony here was that Michel's view seems substantially to have become the view of the Second Vatican Council, specifically of *Sacrosanctum Concilium*, but then largely to have failed of implementation. In many ways, what was needed was not the liturgical experimentation of the postconciliar years, but an implementation of the Council document *Sacrosanctum Concilium*, which remains largely untried.

Again, there may be seemingly insurmountable barriers here faced by specific individuals because they find themselves caught in a parish life deeply accommodated to the world. Though of course the liturgy can be celebrated in many settings, its usual home is the parish. The parish is the context in which most Christians live their lives and is the clear alternative to either an isolated or a sectarian existence.

---

[59] Keith F. Pecklers, *The Unread Vision: The Liturgical Movement in the United States of America: 1926–1955* (Collegeville, Minn.: Liturgical Press, 1998), 132, quoted in a review by Kurt Belsole in *Antiphon* 4, no. 1 (1999): 33–34 at 34. The parallel work of Michel and Day is described throughout Peckler's book. See also Mark and Louise Zwick, "Dorothy Day and the Catholic Worker Movement", the introduction to Dorothy Day, *On Pilgrimage* (Grand Rapids, Mich.: W. B. Eerdmans, 1999), 1–64.

It must continue to be the womb of Christian identity, along with the family. We need in regard to the latter to be much more attentive to domestic ritual. In the words of Andrew Ciferni, "The keeping of times and seasons in prayer, and symbolic acts in the home, is another example of what is perhaps the most crucial pastoral challenge of our day, inculturation."[60] When we speak of inculturation our heads must not in the first instance be filled with global plans; our thought must begin with our homes and parishes. "Without suitable and appropriate domestic rituals . . . the effectiveness of the formal rites will be severely limited. Domestic rituals have been in the past more crucial in mediating and establishing a rich Catholic spirituality . . . than we have been willing to admit."[61] The movie *Waking Ned Devine*, with its various blessings, illustrates this very well.

Let me suggest the possibilities of domestic ritual by one of my married daughters' story of saying the Angelus at home. My daughter lives within hearing distance of the bells of her parish church. When her firstborn had just begun to walk, my daughter began to say the Angelus with her when the bells rang at 6:00 P.M., using a pretty blue prayer book from the National Shrine. The second time she was preparing to do this, when the bells rang she asked her daughter, "What do the bells mean?" The child ran to get the prayer book, although perhaps she was interested only in the book itself. Eventually as soon as my granddaughter heard the bells, she ran to get the book without any prompting. By age two, if

---

[60] Andrew Ciferni, "The Need for Domestic Rituals", *Priests and People* 11, no. 2 (Feb. 1997): 45, cited in Cummings, "How Adequate Are the Post-conciliar Catholic Funeral Rites", 22.

[61] Cummings, "How Adequate Are the Postconciliar Catholic Funeral Rites", 22, who is speaking specifically of funeral rites.

asked, "What do the bells mean?" she answered, "Prayers."
Clearly, this little prayer had become a part of her life, and
she already was living by a cycle of prayer.

Serious attention must be paid so that all that is corrupt-
ing in secular culture does not fatally wound the family, and
with it the parish:[62]

> Young people are increasingly citizens of an autonomous
> country. Even if living at home, by the age of eleven their
> spirits are dwelling elsewhere. While their values are obvi-
> ously influenced by television, even more potent is the tem-
> per of popular music, in which, it should be added, rap has
> only a very small part. The advertising industry and fast-
> food chains—the latter competing with the family dinner
> table—have done much to create this nation which young
> people find so alluring.

These are not the words of some conservative commentator,
but of Andrew Hacker, writing in the *New York Review of
Books.* Being a parent continues to become more and more
difficult, and unless Catholic parents are taught to think of
the family as something consciously countercultural, and the
parish can offer a life more wholesome and attractive than
that pandered by popular culture at every step, there hardly
can be a human, let alone a Catholic, future.[63] Parents must
have a consciously determined policy regarding television, if
it is allowed into the home at all. They must be taught that

---

[62] Andrew Hacker, "The War over the Family", *The New York Review of
Books* 44, no. 19 (Dec. 4, 1997): 34–38 at 36–37.

[63] In an obvious sense, the liturgy itself is now countercultural: John Paul II
remarked in an address of Oct. 9, 1998, to the bishops of the Northwestern
United States, printed in *Antiphon* 3, no. 3 (1998): 29–31 at 30: "In a culture
which neither favors nor fosters meditative quiet, the art of interior listening
is learned only with difficulty. Here we see how the liturgy, though it must
always be properly inculturated, must also be countercultural."

part of preparation for marriage is discussion of such issues and coming to shared conclusions about them. In some ways the constant rousing of adolescent—and not simply adolescent—sexual urges by prime-time television is the least of the problem. More insidious is the constant advertising of expensive, unnecessary products made out to be necessities. How can we expect parents to stay home with their children if the message commercial culture gives them is that every family needs to have more money to buy such "necessities", so both parents must work?

As I have said, in specific instances the reinvigoration of parish life may be very difficult, so difficult that some other conception of community will, for at least some, be a more suitable vehicle for achieving an unreserved Christian life.[64] There is the possibility of life attached to one of the ecclesial movements such as Communion and Liberation. Many of these continue to flourish, loving the world, but opposing what is not ordered to God. In a talk delivered on the Vigil of Pentecost in 1998 in Saint Peter's Square, John Paul remarked that with the Second Vatican Council the Church recovered her charismatic dimension.[65] Following on this has been a remarkable growth in the ecclesial movements. These provide alternatives to the secularized models of life disconnected from God found in the larger culture and, in a highly mobile and fragmented civilization, formation beyond what the average parish can give.

---

[64] Of course I do not mean to suggest that one makes decisions for a specific form of the Christian life (simply) on the basis of the kind of criteria considered here.

[65] Sheila Gribben Liaugminas, "A Renewed Pentecost: Catholic Movements called to 'A New Dynamism'", *Voices* 13, no. 4 (Dec. 1998): 17–19, for this and the following.

In another time of crisis the Jesuits observed that what were needed were a few good men, quality more than quantity, that the world could be changed through a few lives transparent to the will of God. As it turned out, it took more than a few men, but the world really was changed. Something like this is what Radical Orthodoxy and similar theological responses to the crisis of the age envisage. Proponents of these movements do not give up on the world or retreat into a sectarian stance. They wish to engage life as it is today, but from within a believing community, not in heroic isolation. They agree with the *communio* theologians, among whom John Paul is to be numbered, that Christian life in imitation of the life of the Trinity must be social or relational and that we best respond to a hostile culture by offering it an alternative vision of social life restored in Christ. Because such theologians tend to acknowledge that few political orders or states remain Christian in any meaningful sense, least of all some supposedly "Christian America", they reconfigure the relation of Christianity to society so that the Christian is more supported by an individual parish, an ecclesial movement, or the universal patrimony of the faith than by his national culture. They root Christianity in the Church rather than in the nation-state.

There is another response possible here, or rather an important variation on the insistence that Church, not state, form our basic loyalties. For this we return to Cardinal Ouellet, who, without detriment to the idea that the parish must be important in our thinking about the formation of Christian identity, has given special attention to the formation of small contemplative communities remaining in the world but bearing witness to the whole glorious Christian faith, not by moralizing, but by "staying in place" and living the fullness of the gospel. What Cardinal Ouellet desires is the pedagogy of evangelization formulated by Hans Urs von Balthasar.[66] This is based, not on some calculation that it is most unlikely that even a single parish would embrace an unreserved Christian life, but on an almost inverse belief, that since all are called to perfection, communities that embody a wholehearted response to Christ must exist "in the world", where most people are. These communities therefore are not contemplative, if by that one means "world fleeing". They are contemplative in the sense of Saint Basil, or of von Balthasar, or of the sections on prayer of *The Catechism of the Catholic Church*, to which we will turn in the appendixes to this book. Prayer and contemplation are understood to be the means by which one orients oneself to God and man, therefore to life "in the world".

Traditionally the decision to live the trinitarian life without reservation expressed itself in the monastic life or by joining a religious order, but the Balthasarian point is that, since all are called to unreserved life in Christ "in but not of the world", an appropriate contemporary response is Christians who stay in their worldly place and strive for perfection there. Hence the houses of Saint John, communities of those who have taken vows but who remain in the city and in customary forms of work. The Christian's "duty is to experience the presence of absolute love, and himself to actualise it, and to make it visible, within his love for his neighbour".[67] The Christian is to offer a concept of love different from that slightly still-warm ember of love the contemporary world sometimes calls "relationships". He is to manifest a contemplative love ori-

---

[66] "Jesus Christ, the One Savior", 225, 232. See above all Balthasar's *Love Alone*, trans. Alexander Dru (New York: Herder and Herder, 1969).

[67] Hans Urs von Balthasar, "Our Christian Inheritance and the Christian Task", *The Glory of the Lord: A Theological Aesthetics*, vol. 5: *The Realm of Metaphysics in the Modern Age*, ed. Oliver Davies et al., trans. Brian McNeil and John Riches (San Francisco: Ignatius Press, 1991), 613–36.

ented to God and shared with his neighbor. This is not the same
as the response of the ecclesial orders or of Radical Orthodoxy to today's world, but a parallel proposal as to what evangelization might look like in the new millennium.

I have suggested that contemporary culture is not simply
on a one-way track to an ever-increasing secularization defined as the removal of life from God. Rather, as in all ages,
a struggle is going on between various forms of secularization and various forms of sacralization. I also have suggested
that there is a dialectic present in culture in which undesirable developments deepen understanding, God in this sense
bringing good from evil. I would like to close by illustrating
this through consideration of the analysis of Modernity by
the Italian thinker Augusto del Noce (1910–1989). Another
Italian writer has summarized del Noce's position thus:[68]

> Modernity cannot simply be equated with secularization and
> the atheism towards which it tends, but also includes a re-
> action to this process that deepens the tradition. Modernity
> is not to be equated with a race towards atheism but, if any-
> thing, the sorting out of two alternative positions: transcen-
> dence versus atheism. Atheism is not the destiny of the West,
> but its problem, and the key to understanding modern man
> is not Nietzsche's death of God, but Pascal's wager.

That is, the development of Modernity allows us to see more
adequately what is at issue in the alternatives of a life ordered
by atheism and one ordered by transcendence.

Del Noce distinguished between two kinds of thinkers in
the modern period, whom he called the rationalist thinker

---

[68] Giuseppe Riconda, "Augusto Del Noce: Between Thomism and Religious Existentialism", *Communio* 25 (1998): 716–31 at 720, for the quotation
and what follows.

and the religious thinker. The rationalist considers reason to be unproblematic, a kind of calculating tool, used to quantify, to pass from premise to premise, and to judge syllogisms. Its meaning and use seem as clear or transparent to the rationalist as that of any Cartesian "clear and distinct idea". He does not understand himself to have opted for a specific notion of reason, that is, that there are other, fuller, definitions available. Any such choice he has made is hidden from him, much in the way that Karl Löwith noted that in the modern period almost all historical thought has been grounded in theological assumptions, but that only the Christian historians have seen this.[69] To use Alasdair MacIntyre's way of making a point similar to Del Noce's, the rationalist does not realize that he stands in a tradition constructed by a myriad of choices and that neither he nor anything about his tradition is unproblematic.[70] He expresses the confidence of Modernity, not the second thoughts of Postmodernity. Further, he does not take the doctrine of original sin seriously and assumes that reason as he finds it is not scarred. By contrast, the religious thinker of the modern period, typified by Pascal (1623–1662), knows that he chooses. By this much he has a critical superiority to the rationalist and, we might add, is the natural ally of postmodernity in its attack on such ideas as an unqualified objectivity. No object may be viewed except from within a tradition.

The irony, as usual contradicting the stereotypes so dear and necessary to liberalism, is that in the modern period the religious thinker understood that his life was a wager, while the rationalist spoke dogmatically, thus all the assertions with-

---

[69] *Meaning in History* (Chicago: University of Chicago Press, 1949).

[70] *Three Rival Versions of Moral Enquiry: Encyclopaedia, Genealogy, and Tradition* (Notre Dame, Ind.: University of Notre Dame, 1990).

out possibility of appeal, epitomized by Nietzsche's "God is dead." Without such dogmatic assertions one could not know which side was history's side; one could not be modern. One would have to acknowledge that history was no more transparent than reason. One could not be privy to the history of being. One's description of religion as out of step with history was revealed as mere bluster and the declaration that one could organize life without God as a mere power play on man's behalf. Del Noce's genius was that he saw that what the modern period called atheism was not some scientific conclusion that good argument had established, but something absolutely willful, the logical precondition for the kind of world the rationalist wished. The rationalist could not have the kind of world he wanted without the rejection of God; therefore "God [was] dead." If the nature of atheist dogmatism long was unperceived by its practitioners, Marx, when he declared that God *must not* exist, finally achieved some understanding of the arbitrariness of such thought. This came to full term in the combination of cynicism and smugness found in Sartre's statement that "existentialism is not the sort of atheism that consists simply in demonstrating that God does not exist. It rather declares that, even if God did exist, nothing would change." [71] The kind of sad incapacity for critical thought thus revealed consisted in observing that the dogmatism of rationalist thought had through repetition become so ingrained that it no longer needed defense.

The most terrible thing about atheism is its rejection of transcendence, first of all of the idea that the human reason is the image of God and not simply a tool for various this-worldly operations. That is, while the reason can do all the

[71] Riconda, "Augusto Del Noce", 720–21 at 721 for Sartre.

things rationalists asked of it in the modern period, the religious man saw it as something more, as one of those spiritual capacities for transcendence, for orientation to God, which, for instance, make the life of prayer possible. He followed Augustine in seeing that we are made for God. An overriding Christian task of the twenty-first century will be revealing all the arbitrariness of the rationalist's narrowing of the meaning of reason in the modern period, a narrowing that made possible the instinctive identification of reason with the category "brain" in so much modern thought, rather than with the categories "soul" or "spirit".[72] Here the Church has no choice, as she pursues a resacralization of intelligence, than to be a sign of contradiction. Del Noce suggests that to do this "the problem of religion needs to be framed in terms of choice and wager".[73]

Thus Pascal, who of course has not exactly flourished in the courses on philosophy, becomes Modernity's great sign of contradiction.[74] The question is whether, with Pascal, we can return really to viewing the human condition under the headings of both image of God and original sin, to see man as "a thinking reed". The past few centuries have been filled with so many forms of perfectionism that have tried to ignore original sin that it is now difficult, for instance, to know what a politics that takes original sin seriously would look like. Del Noce takes

[72] Warren S. Brown, Nancey Murphy, and H. Newton Malony, eds., *Whatever Happened to the Soul? Scientific and Theological Portraits of Human Nature* (Minneapolis: Fortress Press, 1998). Edward Pols, *Mind Regained* (Ithaca, N.Y.: Cornell University Press, 1998), attacks looking only to the brain for explanation of mind. William Hasker, *The Emergent Self* (Ithaca, N.Y.: Cornell University Press, 1999), challenges physicalist views in current philosophy of mind.

[73] Riconda, "Augusto Del Noce", 727, for this and the following.

[74] Marvin R. O'Connell, *Blaise Pascal: Reasons of the Heart* (Grand Rapids, Mich.: W. B. Eerdmans, 1997).

notice of the great Russian religious thinkers who have had something to say about this matter. They, with good reason, have had a marked tendency to view the West as the embodiment of the rationalism Del Noce criticized. But of course Del Noce's point was that the West was characterized not by an inexorable tendency to secularization, but by a dualism in which the tradition of Pascal has made cogent response to the tradition of Descartes and revealed the arbitrary assumptions on which the rationalist tradition stands. We can now see that modesty demands of all the abandonment of unqualified notions of objectivity and the acceptance of the fact that no one can think except from within a tradition. Religious thinkers have often been as naive about such questions as rationalists have been, the Catholic as much as the rationalist identifying reason with the operations studied in a logic course.

In sum, secularization, removal of life from God, has been accompanied by a deepening of understanding so that it is precisely in the West, more than among the great Russian religious thinkers studied by Del Noce, that Christians have worked out the implications of the abandonment of transcendence.[75] For those who wish to see, the dialectical development of the civilization has revealed much more clearly than ever before what is at issue in choosing for or against God. It has shown that a future without God is not something inevitable, but something one chooses.[76] Augustine once said that the times will

---

[75] Riconda, "Augusto Del Noce", 730–32.

[76] Cf. John Milbank, Catherine Pickstock, and Graham Ward, eds., *Radical Orthodoxy: A New Theology* (London: Routledge, 1999), introduction, 1: "For several centuries now, secularism has been defining and constructing the world ... in its early manifestations secular Modernity exhibited anxiety concerning its own lack of ultimate ground—the scepticism of Descartes, the cynicism of Hobbes, the circularities of Spinoza all testify to this ... today the logic of secularism is imploding."

be what we ourselves choose to be, and that remains so. Even the rationalists can now see much of the damage done by their position. In secularizing the world, it was not just God who was isolated. Mother nature, who had formerly been *mater*, became matter, unendingly to be manipulated by reason because severed from God and God's designs. The severing of the created order from God typically involved the notion that there is no truth of creation, no plan of God for life, not even an organic structure proper to each creature that must be respected.[77] Though those caught in Modernity—say, the scientists who "create life in a dish"—continue to inhabit the space created by severing nature from God, others have become very nervous about this, some ecologists going so far as to say that only piety will save the environment. The discovery of the laws of nature, as Newton himself had hoped, could have encouraged piety and led to seeing all existence as theophanous. Man's task could have been seen as a "methaphysics of wholeness", the integration of the old and the new, the placement of man as spirit within a natural order that was relinquishing its secrets. Instead, man's spiritual nature was increasingly denuded, reduced to being merely another instance of matter in motion. We may close by seconding Hans Urs von Balthasar's proposal that the Christian task now is to take up this uncompleted work of integration: "This is the ultimate truth: that Christians, as guardians of a metaphysics of the whole person in an age which has forgotten both Being and God, are entrusted with the weighty responsibility of leading this metaphysics of wholeness through that same fire [of testing]."[78]

---

[77] I am working here and in what follows from a privately printed "Arkwood Foundation" statement of principles supplied to me by David L. Schindler.

[78] Balthasar, "Our Christian Inheritance", 654–55 at 655.

APPENDIX ONE

Prayer as Relation in the
Catechism of the Catholic Church

In regard to the pedagogy of evangelization promoted by Hans Urs von Balthasar, Chapter Five made passing reference to prayer and contemplation as treated in the *Catechism of the Catholic Church* as the means of orientation to God and to life "in the world". In this Appendix, I would like to explore this understanding, which also allows us to view ideas about history and temporal development introduced in earlier chapters in fuller perspective. Part IV of the *Catechism of the Catholic Church* (no. 2558) defines prayer as "vital and personal relationship with the living and true God" of a person living the mystery of the faith.[1] Prayer is relationship. This is a very profound definition that stresses that we are beings the fullness of whose existence is expressed in prayer. Aristotle was right to call us rational animals, but the mystery of faith helps us understand that we are much more than this. We are praying animals.

Americans and many others are commonly brought up in a tradition of individualism well illustrated by the myth of the

---

[1] *Catechism of the Catholic Church*, 2nd ed. (Vatican City: Libreria Editrice Vaticana, 2000). Cf. throughout the reflections of Christoph Schönborn, *Living the Catechism of the Catholic Church*, vol. 4: *Paths of Prayer* (San Francisco: Ignatius Press, 2003).

social contract.[2] Autonomy rather than relationship is the central concern. Instinctively focus is on the individual as the basic unit of society, and society is understood as constructed by consenting autonomous individuals who each agree to give up a bit of their autonomy to create the state or government. Implicit is the idea that each person is a Cartesian individual, an independent self-conscious locus of intellect and will. As adults we indeed in some degree do become this, but it does not take much reflection to see that such a way of picturing ourselves is most incomplete and superficial.

None of us starts out as a self-conscious, autonomous individual. We start out in utter dependency, in relationship, first to our mothers, but also to a whole world around us.[3] It takes us years to figure out where the latter ends and we begin. What appears a kind of self-centeredness in small children, in which each thinks that what he desires is the sum total of reality, is in fact the expression of an inability clearly to separate the self from the world. This may be viewed in various ways: as an inability to see that there is anything but one's self, an inability to draw clear boundaries between one's self and other persons or things, or an inability to perceive that there are bounds placed on one's own self by the existence of a world of objects and other selves. Only slowly is the child able to understand that there are other subjects, other egos, making claims and that these help to define himself.

---

[2] Glenn W. Olsen, "John Rawls and the Flight from Authority: The Quest for Equality as an Exercise in Primitivism", *Interpretation: A Journal of Political Philosophy* 21 (1994): 419–36.

[3] David L. Schindler, "Creation and Nuptiality: A Reflection on Feminism in Light of Schmemann's Liturgical Theology", *Communio: International Catholic Review* 28 (2001): 265–95 at 283, develops the idea that relations (partly) constitute human persons.

Left to himself, the newborn soon dies. He survives only because he is born in relationship, into a family. Being born in relationship is not something accidental; it is part of our definition. We are someone's child, and we will be defined by this fact forever. Though each of us has something unique about himself—this is a truth that individualism is both built on and distorts—we are social beings, born in and for relationship. The communion of persons that we call a family not only, rather than the individual, is the basic unit of society, but also provides a context that defines the individual and allows him to come to consciousness. Rather than starting out as self-conscious, we only slowly rise to consciousness of how from the beginning we have been in relations that define us. In the same process we discover what is unique and what relational about ourselves.

The great insight of trinitarian theology is that the whole universe, God included, is so constituted. The Trinity is not three isolated Persons, but three Persons in relation. Without the relations, they would not be Persons. All that defines or is unique to each Divine Person is his relation to the others: everything else is shared, of one substance. Father, Son, and Spirit are equally God, but only the Father is Father, and the Son Son. From eternity, the Son has always been Son of the Father, and the Father Father of the Son. These are not interchangeable roles. Rather, because from the beginning the Son had from the Father the mission of being sent to the world, his Person was always defined by obedience, just as the Person of the Father was defined by the authority to command.[4]

---

[4] Javier Prades, "The Tribe or the Global Village? Fundamental Reflections on Multiculturalism", *Communio* 28 (2001): 348–76 at 368–69, excellently discusses mission in relation to mutual love.

Whether in the Trinity or between God and man, if prayer is relationship with God, it is what constitutes all being. The intercommunion of Father, Son, and Spirit is prayer, and so is our relation to God. As Cardinal Ratzinger has expressed it, "Christian praying ... is the response one freedom makes to another freedom, an encounter of love." [5] We find our very being in prayer; it is the state in which we were made to be. Aristotle saw that we are defined by our ability to speak, and Christianity helps us understand that we are defined by our ability, in prayer, to speak with the source of our being. To use a current idiom, we are programmed to pray.

We tend to take for granted or even fail to observe the many ways we have been programmed by and for God. Conscience as the foundation of the moral life is perhaps the most obvious of these. We did not make conscience; we cannot control it, except in the sense of silencing or dimming it. Conscience is a gift from God that, as John Henry Newman saw, at least partially defines our person. It is God in us directing and calling us back to himself, the Creator calling to the created. Augustine was not wrong to structure his thought around the two great realities, God and the soul. God calls out to the soul, and the soul to God, and this reciprocal call is prayer. Thus no. 2591 of the *Catechism* says, "Prayer unfolds throughout the whole history of salvation as a reciprocal call between God and man."

By the very fact that we are created beings, we are established in relation to God in other ways. I once reviewed a book by a Catholic in which evil was equated with suffer-

⁵ Joseph Cardinal Ratzinger, *Turning Point for Europe? The Church in the Modern World—Assessment and Forecast*, trans. Brian McNeil (San Francisco: Ignatius Press, 1994), 110.

ing.[6] Is not suffering, rather, at least in part, another of those things that speak of our orientation to God? Simone Weil thought suffering, along with beauty, one of the two things that draw us up short to force us to ask ultimate questions. Some years ago (*Pascha 1995*) I received the reflections of an eighty-year-old, the abbot of the monastery of the Holy Transfiguration in California, on the occasion of his sixtieth year as a monk of the Eastern Catholic rite. An older brother had approached Father Abbot asking why he, the older brother, had had a life filled with suffering. The response was that suffering is our participation in the cosmic "unfinishedness". This recalled Paul's remark about filling up the suffering of Christ. As created and therefore finite beings, we are made for perfection and for life with the Perfect. Suffering under its many forms is our participation in a struggle that will last until God is all in all. Loneliness, for instance, in each of its concrete forms is an expression of the fact that we have not yet come to rest in a Heart, Other, or Love that satisfies. Jesus said (Mt 11:28), "Come to me, all you who labour and are overburdened, and I will give you rest" (Jerusalem Bible translation). Thus, as well as conscience, suffering is a means by which we find our path back to God. It is a measure of "unfinishedness".

An underlying theme of the *Catechism* is that morality, mysticism, liturgy, and all other dimensions of Catholic existence are expressions of prayer, aspects of our relation to God. Thus the striking expression in Part III, no. 2031, "*The moral life is spiritual worship.* We 'present [our] bodies as a living sacrifice, holy and acceptable to God.'" Here, quoting Romans 12:1, the moral life is seen as liturgical or Eucharistic.

---

[6] *Thought* 53 (1978): 226–27.

That is, to live the moral life in Christ is a form of living sacrifice. Further, no. 2031 continues, "In the liturgy and the celebration of the sacraments, prayer and teaching are conjoined with the grace of Christ to enlighten and nourish Christian activity. As does the whole of the Christian life, the moral life finds its source and summit in the Eucharistic sacrifice." That is, above all in the Eucharistic sacrifice, prayer, doctrine, and morals are conjoined, and each nurses the others. All liturgy has an eschatological orientation in which "the liturgy of earth . . . [is] carried into the trinitarian embrace of the liturgy of heaven." [7] (See also the *Catechism*, no. 1084ff.) Indeed, though this is not the focus of our discussion here, one can reasonably assert that "the most startling thing about the liturgical theology of the new Catechism . . . is its dramatic reassertion of the cosmic dimension of Christian worship." [8]

Prayer as the way back to the Love who has made us often is intimately related to suffering and struggle. Number 2573 of the *Catechism* says of Jacob's wrestling (Gen 32:24–30) all night with a mysterious figure who turns out to be God: "From this account, the spiritual tradition of the Church has retained the symbol of prayer as a battle of faith and as the triumph of perseverance." Number 2612 describes the dis-

---

[7] M. Francis Mannion, "A New Phase of Liturgical Reform", *Antiphon: Publication of the Society for Catholic Liturgy* 5, no. 1 (2000): 2–4 at 3. In the same issue, 23–31, Aidan Nichols, "A Tale of Two Documents: *Sacrosanctum Concilium* and *Mediator Dei*", develops the theme of eschatological consciousness, particularly commending Jean Corbon, *The Wellspring of Worship* (Nahwah, N.J.: Paulist Press, 1988). Corbon, of the Centre des Dominicains in Beirut, was the author of the concluding book, the section on prayer reflected on here, of the *Catechism of the Catholic Church*.

[8] M. Francis Mannion, "Bringing the Cosmos to Liturgy", *Antiphon* 6, no. 1 (2001): 2–4 at 3.

ciples' prayer as a battle and says that "only by keeping watch in prayer can one avoid falling into temptation." The alert person knows he is constantly tempted and must stand guard on himself. I remember years ago my wife and I sitting on a beach in Minnesota with another couple. Our and their young children were in the water. We adults were engaged in conversation and banter, but constantly our eyes surveyed the surface of the water, as mentally we each repetitively ticked off to ourself the number of our children. This had become such a habit, one expression of the job description of being a parent, that is, of never completely relaxing, that I was hardly aware of it until the wife of the other couple wondered aloud if the time would ever come when she could apply her mind to something more significant than counting from one to three. Hard truths are that we must be watchful in many things and that prayer is a form of watchfulness. The more alive we are, the more we realize that struggle and suffering are at the heart of existence. Only slackers breeze through life and fail to note that we are constantly faced with temptations and choices to be dealt with in watchful prayer. One of the forms of praying without ceasing is never letting down one's guard.

Each of us has a mission that expresses our relation to God, and prayer is a dialogue with God about the nature of that mission.[9] In a few words no. 2576, speaking of Moses, goes to the heart of the matter. Exodus 33:11 tells us that "the Lord used to speak to Moses face to face, as a man speaks to

---

[9] William T. Cavanaugh, "Balthasar, Globalization, and the Problem of the One and the Many", *Communio* 28 (2001): 324–47 at 343–47, reflects on the relation between our shared humanity and our individual uniqueness or mission, specifically in regard to Hans Urs von Balthasar, *Theo-Drama: Theological Dramatic Theory*, vol. 3: *Dramatis personae: Persons in Christ*, trans. Graham Harrison (San Francisco: Ignatius Press, 1992), 51.

his friend." Then the *Catechism* adds, "Moses' prayer is characteristic of contemplative prayer by which God's servant remains faithful to his mission." Contemplative prayer in this context is a "face-to-face" prayer, a form of conversation that does not so much ask something of God, at least for oneself (2577 notes Moses "does not pray for himself but for the people whom God made his own"), as "look at" God to clarify one's mission. Just as Jesus was sent by the Father into the world with a mission, so each of us receives a mission.[10] To have a mission is to come from somewhere for some purpose, and to remain faithful to a mission is to keep in mind its origin. Contemplative prayer in this context is reflection on God as the source of our mission. It is something that, like doctrine, must be lived out in our lives if it is to be real.

This is what von Balthasar meant when he said that liturgy and contemplation unite us to the source from which we have come. Contemplative prayer ties together the sacred half of life, which we experience most intensely in the Mass, and the secular half of life of our workaday world. There is a sense in which the Mass attended in the morning fades as the day progresses, as we engage in worldly labor. It almost seems that we must choose between the sacred and the secular; none of us can remain with the Eucharist all day long. It is contemplation, prayer that reflects on the mysteries of the faith, that mediates between these two halves of life, that ties them together intrinsically. Instead of a mere juxtaposition of the sacred and the secular, contemplative prayer allows a joining of these two. We walk away from Mass or are

[10] Cavanaugh, "Balthasar, Globalization, and the Problem of the One and the Many", 344, develops the idea that human existence "is receptivity to being sent out". See in the same issue Prades, "Tribe or the Global Village?" at 363–64, on our "being-in-community".

sent into our everyday world while remaining connected to the source of our being. Contemplative prayer—this too is prayer without ceasing—allows us to keep our eschatological bearing. In words from von Balthasar's book *Prayer,*[11] contemplation "instructs ... [us] how to live on earth in the spirit of heaven".

This is why at all costs a narrow view of prayer must be avoided. Prayer must not be identified with only one set of practices. It is as multiform as communication or speech itself. A shrug of the shoulders, a nod of the head, is as much speech as something that comes out of the mouth or flows from a pen. Thus, the first paragraph of Part IV of the *Catechism* (no. 2558) closes with a statement of Saint Thérèse of Lisieux: "For me, prayer is a surge of the heart; it is a simple look turned toward heaven, it is a cry of recognition and of love, embracing both trial and joy." Here Thérèse also thinks of prayer as relation to God. It can as well be expressed in a surge of the heart or a look turned toward heaven as in any word. Thérèse sees that prayer not so much expresses our relation to God as lives in that relation. Prayer is so well described as a surge of the heart because the heart cannot desire its object unless it already is in relation to that object. To give a simple look toward heaven is the expression of a habitual sense that we are heaven oriented. We may leave home and loved ones at the beginning of the workday, but in a profound sense, in the degree they remain in our thoughts, we never leave them. At the end of the day, the simple greeting of return is an expression of a relation that has been there

---

[11] Hans Urs von Balthasar, *Prayer*, trans. Graham Harrison (San Francisco: Ignatius Press, 1986), see especially pp. 99–107. The citation was quoted in the *Houston Catholic Worker* 15 (April 1995): 6, by followers of Dorothy Day who are still trying to keep the two halves of life intrinsically related.

all day long. A "simple look toward our spouse" brings once again to the center of consciousness something always there, but for a time, because of our preoccupation with our daily labor, "only" in the background. This is Thérèse's world. Whatever the Christian does, what defines him is his relation to God. Although prayer may be a form of bringing what is always in the background to the foreground, it may be no more than articulating the fact that there is a background. Thus the simple look toward heaven.

The goal is always to see things from heaven's point of view. Thus in Part III of the *Catechism*, no. 2157 urges, "The Christian begins his day, his prayers, and his activities with the Sign of the Cross: 'in the name of the Father and of the Son and of the Holy Spirit. Amen.' The baptized person dedicates the day to the glory of God and calls on the Savior's grace which lets him act in the Spirit as a child of the Father. The sign of the cross strengthens us in temptations and difficulties." The prayerful person is the person who habitually considers the relations between God and the world, thinks of his everyday life as in relation to God. Sacramentals and brief prayers through the day draw one's look toward heaven.

A Byzantine miniature painted about 1059 A.D., showing Christ turned in prayer to the Father, is printed in the *Catechism* just preceding Part IV. It expresses the simple look toward heaven. The caption directs the reader to no. 2599, where Jesus is said to have learned "the formulas of prayer from his mother, who kept in her heart and meditated upon all the 'great things' done by the Almighty." This idea of treasuring something in one's heart is like the simple look toward heaven. It is not so much a formal prayer, certainly not a prayer of petition, as a meditation on the work of salvation itself, God's gift to the world. In the miniature, Christ looks up to the heavens and to the Father from whom he has come, that is, orients himself in this world by his relation to the Father. In no. 2599 Mary asks for nothing, makes no petition, but simply reflects on what God has done, how he has expressed his relation to us.

In the same paragraph, in regard to Jesus' words at twelve years of age, we are told that "the newness of prayer in the fullness of time begins to be revealed." Christ announces and brings a Kingdom. Number 2612 quotes Mark 1:15: "In Jesus 'the Kingdom of God is at hand.'" Number 2607, to which the caption of the Byzantine miniature directs us as the context in which to understand Peter's pointing to Christ as the Master of prayer, speaks of "the newness of the coming Kingdom". The relation in which as creatures we stand to our Creator is immeasurably clarified by Christ entering our world and announcing the coming Kingdom. Christ in prayer announces proper relation to God.

Our world has been disordered by sin and is never adequately in proper relation to God. Again, Thérèse of Lisieux (in no. 2558) exclaims prayer "is a cry of recognition and of love, embracing both trial and joy". That is, it is a love expressed from here below. Because we live in a world disordered by sin, but of which Christ has begun the transfiguration, we at once experience "trial and joy". Prayer of petition is a response to trial, prayer of adoration to joy. These are the two forms of prayer concisely described in the *Catechism*'s quotation from Saint John Damascene at no. 2590: "Prayer is the raising of one's mind and heart to God or the requesting of good things from God." [12] There are other forms of prayer, but perhaps these two stand at the poles, the one

[12] The CCC is quoting St. John Damascene, *De fide orth.* 3, 24: PG 94, 1089C.

oriented to things we need, the other centered directly on God. So long as we live here below, both forms of prayer will be proper. Christ comes to announce an order in which God's will will be done, in which joy will triumph. But that order is only appearing in the midst of an order that is dying. Christ announces a Kingdom in which all, like himself, turn toward the Father. He announces the Kingdom in which God's will will be done. When Peter asks him, "Lord, teach us to pray", the prayer he receives, the Lord's Prayer, the prayer to which Part IV of the *Catechism* builds, is a prayer for those still in this world, who nevertheless look toward heaven.

Here Christ is the Master of prayer. The *Catechism*, Part I (no. 741) used this expression, "master of prayer", to describe the Holy Spirit, in the process preparing the way for giving Christ the same title in Part IV. Number 741 begins by quoting Romans 8:26: "The Spirit helps us in our weakness; for we do not know how to pray as we ought, but the Spirit himself intercedes with sighs too deep for words." In part this is Thérèse's idea that prayer may be something other than or more than words. As in Peter's request in Luke that he be taught to pray, the idea in Romans is that we do not, at least adequately, know how to pray. The message of Luke and Romans is that prayer is a gift in a radical sense. We are so weak and confused that we cannot pray properly, and so the Spirit prays for us. And the Spirit's language is like that of Thérèse, one of "sighs too deep for words". Most parents have known the misery of watching a child at least in danger of losing his way. Certainly such parents' fear may be put in words, but what move in their prayer are "sighs too deep for words". What counts is not so much what is said, but the whole inclination of the person who prays.

In answering the question "what is prayer?" the *Catechism* defines prayer as three things: gift, covenant, and communion. The presentation of prayer as gift is very arresting. Number 2560 places the reader in the position of the Samaritan woman by beginning with Jesus' exclamation to her in John 4:10 following his request for a drink: "If you knew the gift of God!" The "wonder of prayer" is that "Christ comes to meet every human being." Always the emphasis is on the initiative of God, on the Spirit who sighs wordlessly: "It is he who first seeks us and asks us for a drink. Jesus thirsts; his asking arises from the depths of God's desire for us." Here, behind the human thirst of Jesus, we see the divine thirst, which is desire that we desire him: "Whether we realize it or not, prayer is the encounter of God's thirst with ours. God thirsts that we may thirst for him." Jesus then (no. 2561) tells the Samaritan woman that he could have given her living water. What we take to be our need, our petition, is already God in us moving us to him.

The treatment of prayer as covenant, as everything in the *Catechism*, expresses the common faith of the Church, but also builds on themes that Pope John Paul II has made especially his own. The statement (in no. 2562) that "it is the whole man who prays" is one of these and expresses John Paul's theology of the body. This is not developed at this point in the *Catechism*, but brief elaboration is in order. One idea of John Paul and the *Catechism* is that, because we are composites of body and soul, both body and soul pray. Our bodies express attitudes as much as do our souls. In an obvious sense, they do this more than our souls. Saint Bernard, following monastic tradition, saw very far here, with his insistence that our bodies mirror our souls. Just as the sun shines through clouds, our soul expresses itself in the postures and gestures of our bodies. Actually, although the imagery of sun shining through cloud came from the Neoplatonic tradition, Bernard's preferred language was not that of body and soul at all: like the *Catechism* here (2562), he loved to speak of the heart as what prays. "Heart" is the (first Jewish and then) Christianized term for the composite body/soul that prays.[13]

The Byzantine miniature we have been analyzing illustrates the fact that religious art has normally seen the importance of bodily orientation in prayer. The posture of each figure in the miniature expresses great dignity. The Byzantine civilization from which this miniature comes highly valued asceticism, and in this miniature Christ has retreated into a deserted place to pray. That he has done so and is alone does not mean he is unaware of his dignity expressed in bodily posture. Although the *Catechism* does not discuss this at this point (but see 1159–62), we might note that when Genesis says we are created in the image and likeness of God it refers to our whole corporeal being and not, as some later Jewish and Christian thinkers had it, simply to our incorporeal intelligence, spirit, or soul. We have been so schooled to think of our likeness to God as by definition noncorporeal, since God has no body, as to forget that not only has the Son taken on flesh, "He who has seen me has seen the Father." Jesus, the entire Jesus, is an Icon of the Father.

When Michelangelo painted the ceiling of the Sistine Chapel, he knew that the Father has no body, but how more effectively to show the great dignity of both God and man than, in depicting the creation, to give Adam a muscular arm with which to stretch out toward God's muscular arm reaching toward him? Nothing created adequately portrays or images forth God. But it is very important that, even in periods that had to struggle for a just appreciation of the body, many theologians saw our ability to walk erect, to gaze

---

[13] Glenn W. Olsen, "Twelfth-Century Humanism Reconsidered: The Case of St. Bernard", *Studi Medievali*, 3a Serie, 31 (1990): 27–53.

heavenward, to make love face to face, as expressions of what distinguishes us from the animals and links us to God. Because we share bodiliness with the animals, we can walk on all fours, scour the earth, or have sex like a dog, that is, use our bodies in the ways the other animals do. But unlike them, because our bodies are united to immortal souls, we can carry and use them in ways that point to our divine origin. Our bodies can articulate a praying attitude.

Prayer is not only gift and covenant, the latter of which is only briefly defined at this point in the *Catechism*; it is also communion. Number 2565 says that "the life of prayer is the habit of being in the presence of the thrice-holy God and in communion with him." In light of the manner in which the *Catechism* defines prayer as relation, von Balthasar's earlier suggestion that we view intertrinitarian relations as those of prayer seems prescient.[14] The Father prays the Son and the Son the Father. Prayer is communion, "being-in-the-presence-of". This is why prayer and the mystical life are at root the same. Prayer as communion is taking delight in God. No more than for the lover in the presence of the beloved are words necessary. The lover and the contemplative are content "being-in-the-presence-of". As the Persons of the Trinity rejoice in each other, we rejoice in God.

Chapter One of Part IV of the *Catechism* takes up the revelation of prayer, beginning with the universal call to prayer. Here the *Catechism* works out the idea of God as initiator. God is so profoundly "caller" that as Creator he called us from nothing (2566). For us to exist is to be called of God, called into being and made for him. Only the angels, the

---

[14] On this see Glenn W. Olsen, "Hans Urs von Balthasar and the Rehabilitation of St. Anselm's Doctrine of the Atonement", *Scottish Journal of Theology* 34 (1981): 49–61.

Catechism says, are more capable than we of acknowledging being called. This passing reference to the angels is but one way in which the *Catechism* situates prayer in a fully supernatural context. It certainly is no easier for most moderns to think of themselves as dwelling "in a world of spirits" than it was in the middle of the nineteenth century, when the Oxford Movement set about trying to restore a sense of the supernatural. In a world intolerant of the supernatural, it remains difficult to think of the supernatural as the real world. While still an Anglican, in 1850 John Henry Newman said, "No Christian is so humble but he has Angels to attend him", and he called angels "our fellow workers".[15] He thought the world we live in would eventually be transformed to make the "invisible world" of faith visible: "A world of Saints and Angels, a glorious world, the palace of God, the mountains of the Lord of Hosts, the heavenly Jerusalem, the throne of God and Christ". The world of nature is real, but the perspective of the *Catechism* is that it is only a foretaste of the really real.

The *Catechism* goes on to say that the highest form of prayer is that which gives honor and glory back to the Creator. We are not so disfigured by sin as to be unable to desire him who called us into existence. We have lost our likeness to God, but not being in his image. Though our wills are now disordered so that we no longer act like God or use our freedom properly, even in sin we have not lost that in us which is in God's image. We still are intelligent beings who, though we may abuse what we know, are capable of forming knowledge of the true, good, and beautiful.

---

[15] All quotations from Newman may be found in the article by Stanley L. Jaki, "Angels, Brutes, and the Light of Faith", *Crisis* 13, no. 2 (Feb. 1995): 18–22.

The last sentence of 2566 is particularly important: "All religions bear witness to men's essential search for God." The *Catechism* observes in various ways that man is by nature a religious animal. All men are of their created nature made to desire God. All religions, whether making a specific claim to revelation or not, evidence this. God's covenant (2569–70) is not simply with Abraham and his descendants, but with every human being: God has made an (2569) "indefectible covenant with every living creature". In cultures such as that of the United States, formed in large measure by classical Protestantism, we may easily miss the import of such statements to the effect that man is by nature a religious animal.[16] The perspective of the *Catechism* is that humans are created for God and of their nature oriented to him. Even if they lack a specific revelation, humans pray to and search for God. With the Christian revelation they can place a name on the Source and Goal of their desire, but it is faith and grace, not religion, that are added to nature. We are as much by nature religious animals as we are rational animals.

Ideas have great importance in shaping cultures. The denial of the analogy of being and of natural theology in classical Protestantism has had a profound role in shaping Protestant cultures, which, in rejecting the idea that grace builds on nature—better, penetrates nature—tend to the rejection of the view that humans are by nature religious. In these cultures "religion" is either, where there is some memory of Luther and Calvin, a delusional category of reason

[16] I develop what is said here at length in "Separating Church and State", *Faith and Reason* 20 (1994): 403–25. Using the *Church of the Lukumi Babalu Aye v. City of Hialeah* or Santería case as an example, I try to show how different from any analysis being presently advanced questions of Church and state would look if either natural law or religion as a natural category were taken seriously.

straying or, where the long-term tendency to conflate moral and revelatory categories has worked itself out, as in America, another name for faith.[17] In the latter case, there is hardly a memory of religion as a natural category, and one's "religion" is thought of as something given by revelation that is, by definition, not open to public confirmation or refutation. This is of immense moment for the "naked public square". If, on the one hand, religion is simply something given from the other side and held by faith, it must tend to the private, for men of goodwill and integrity may reject it and should in conscience be able to live in society by their own best lights. Historically the logic of secularization implicit in such a view was hidden or hindered for a long time by the establishment of state religions, a practice carried at the level of individual states into colonial American history. The logic of secularization implicit in the refusal to take religion seriously as a natural category has now moved very far in the direction of creation of a so-called neutral, that is, liberal or naked, public space, in which the principal concern has become preserving the rights of citizens who lack agreement about religious or ultimate questions. If, on the other hand, religion is seen as a natural category, it is as much one of the things the state has an obligation to foster as education, and the question becomes the manner in which, granted the fact of pluralism, this can be done. Accommodation of church and state replaces their separation as a goal.

In one's praying, one has always to take into account the political regime in which one lives. This was the point of a great book that in its title viewed *Prayer as a Political Problem*,

[17] In addition to no. 16 above, I have worked this out in "1492 in the Judgment of the Nations", *Actas del II Congreso "Cultura Europea"* (Pamplona, Spain: Thomson Aranzadi, 1994), 175–81.

because seeing that if man is by nature religious, the most serious question to ask any regime was whether it hindered or fostered prayer.[18] Each aspect of one's own culture helps or hinders the life of prayer, and part of defeat of the devil is to discern the ways in which one's culture has screened or blocked off access to God. No amount of ecumenical good-will should keep us from stating a truth without the acknowledgment of which no remedy is possible for the ways in which God has been bracketed out of American culture by thinking of religion or prayer as merely supernatural categories; the heritage of classical Protestantism, having misconstrued the relation between nature and grace and with it that between politics and prayer, has been terribly destructive. This heritage has, in America, also profoundly reshaped Judaism and Catholicism, as Will Herberg saw.[19] Indeed, what is commonly called liberalism is a "secularized Protestantism" that, after the demise of the Protestant ascendancy, continues its bracketing of prayer as a supernatural category. To make the view of the *Catechism* on man's religious nature available to Americans will take a special act of the imagination, to which we now turn.

[18] Jean Cardinal Danielou, trans. J. R. Kirwan (New York: Sheed and Ward, 1967).

[19] *Protestant, Catholic, Jew: An Essay in American Religious Sociology* (Garden City, N.Y.: Anchor Books, 1955).

Prayer as Covenant Drama in the
Catechism of the Catholic Church

The *Catechism of the Catholic Church*, Part IV, no. 2567, views God's call to man as a call for encounter in prayer. Then it presents the complex idea that "[a]s God gradually reveals himself and reveals man to himself, prayer appears as a reciprocal call, a covenant drama." That God reveals himself is central to the idea of revelation, but the idea that God reveals man to himself is especially to be associated with John Paul II. The *Catechism* presents God's revelatory work not simply as giving information about God and salvation, but as slowly revealing man to himself. Because he is a body, man is a historical being, made to live and discover himself through history. Presumably humans can discover something of what they are "by themselves", but without revelation man always falls short of the self-understanding of which he is capable. By nature we desire and seek for God, but only by revelation do we see the depths of this orientation of a created being to its Creator. Prayer is a "reciprocal call" in which God first calls out for us, but we are also made to call out for him.

The idea that prayer is a covenant drama is even richer. Most commonly, especially in recent centuries, what in the last sentence of 2567 is called the "history of salvation" has been presented in narrative form, as the great deeds, especially worked out in the Old Testament, that God has done to call man to himself. Number 2567 adds to this the idea that prayer is "a reciprocal call, a covenant drama". It invites us, in the manner of Hans Urs von Balthasar, to think of God's presence in time according to the categories of drama, as well as of history, to see God's relation to man as dramatic as well as historical. Such terminology highlights the reciprocity of the relation between God and man. In a great cosmic drama, God is playwright or director, man is the actor.

This is a suggestive way of approaching the subject of human freedom. In any good drama, though the playwright sets the script, or the director tells how he wishes the script delivered, the actor is not a mere puppet, every time repeating the same lines in the same way. The actor assumes a role that has its own logic, and he is forever changing his acting as he reflects on this logic and on his character's situation within the drama. There must be trust between the director and the actor, and their relation is reciprocal, one of constant dialogue over the meaning of the part. Presumably the *Catechism* has something like this in mind when it calls prayer "a reciprocal call, a covenant drama". Prayer is our discussion with the playwright of our place in the drama. This drama is not a mere Aristotelian imitation of the course of a tragic hero, for slowly, through the great events God works, it becomes clear that the drama is centered on the saving work of Christ. Indeed, in Christ the director steps on stage.

Christianity radically deepens the understanding of drama and of the drama in which the race is involved. Drama is now seen, in its tragic form, not merely as the falling from high to low estate that Aristotle analyzed, but as the change of estate that was involved in the Son of God taking on flesh and dying on a Cross. God's work in time reveals a new aesthetic or radically expands earlier aesthetics. It redefines beauty in terms of the descent of Christ from heaven, the emptying of God to become man and die on a Cross for the sins of all, and his Resurrection from the dead and return on high to the Father. Aristotle thought tragedy compassed by the loss of estate, the humiliation of a high-born person. He was not completely wrong, but his pagan categories of overstriving excellence, pride, and fall were too partial to give us a full view of the human drama. The Christian drama raises up into a fuller whole the partial pattern of Aristotelian fall and loss of estate to show in Christ the double movement of descent from and return to the Father, humiliation and glorification. *Comedia* follows tragedy. From the vantage point of the Christian drama, even the patterns of nature, the falling of seed into the ground only to be born again, are anticipatory of an aesthetic in which the first is last, he who loses his life the one who saves it.

Thus God's work in time is as much that of a dramatist as it is that of the author of a narrative story. Perhaps "drama engages the heart" in a way historical narration by itself does not. The world is a stage on which the play of obedience and disobedience, of sin and grace, keeps getting worked out, keeps getting new scripts. Man is called to service, to imitation of Christ's giving of himself for all mankind, but how one may best do this must continually be reimagined, must be imagined for one's self. Especially because of the continuing influence of Enlightenment and nineteenth-century ideas, we instinctively think of history as something progressive. In spite of living in what is probably as hellish a century as the race has experienced, most of us do not seriously doubt the adequacy of progressive categories.[1] By

---

[1] As noted above, my "Christian Philosophy, Christian History: Parallel Ideas?" in *Eternity in Time: Christopher Dawson and the Catholic Idea of History*,

contrast, the Bible does not suggest that within history itself there is some progressive advancement of the race. There has been and can be progress in specific things, in understanding and holiness, for instance, but this has not translated into a generalized improvement of the race. Rather, the Bible's question, quoted in no. 2613, is "when the Son of Man comes, will he find faith on earth?" Its perspective is that history ends in Antichrist and apostasy.

Especially in America we have been so intimidated by liberal and progressive commentators who make fun of evangelical Christians for actually taking such views seriously that we do not very systematically ask whether American life today is more intelligible under the progressive or the Christian reading. In any case, the *Catechism* does not present history as a smooth development, progress, or emergence into the light. It sees history as composed of various efforts, some more and some less successful, to establish a proper covenantal relation between God and man. Job's reflection on the covenantal relation is not passé, does not lose its relevancy with the passing of time, but has a permanent validity in spite of Saint Paul's later treatment of the same subject, Paul's complication of the question by the introduction of new dramatic considerations. The drama Job set has the permanence of any good statement of the human predicament.

Number 2568 introduces the idea that the drama of history is about the loss and regaining of right relation to God. Prayer as relation was there from the beginning, in the first act of creating beings related to God, but it was only with the Fall, that is, by injury to the primordial relation, that Adam and Eve noticed its existence. They did this because

---

ed. Stratford Caldecott and John Morrill (Edinburgh: T. and T. Clark, 1997), 131–50, does seriously call such categories in question.

God cried out, "Where are you? ... What is this that you have done?" This cry runs through the Old Testament until finally it, with the restoration made possible by the coming of Christ, receives its proper response, "Lo, I have come to do your will, O God." Christ as the Second Adam restores the right relation to God, which the first Adam lost.

Number 2569 pursues the story of how various of Adam's successors were "walking with God," that is, were living prayer, but also insists: "This kind of prayer is lived by many righteous people in all religions." This statement continues the perspective of Paul in Romans and of Church Fathers such as Justin Martyr and Irenaeus that God has been at work in all the civilizations and religions and that in them there have been those who have responded to his call, that is, have prayed. For, as was argued in Appendix One, man is by nature religious. God's "indefectible covenant with every living creature" (Gen 9:8–16) extends across the religions. Nevertheless, "it is above all beginning with our father Abraham that prayer is revealed in the Old Testament." Abraham's going forth was an act of submission to the call he had heard. The *Catechism* (no. 2570) points out that what was central here was not anything Abraham said. He in fact was silent: "Abraham's prayer is expressed first by deeds.... Only later does Abraham's first prayer in words appear." Thus Abraham's story is a "drama of prayer", a "test of faith in the fidelity of God".

The point of view running through the *Catechism* is that of typology and the Church Fathers. The Covenant with Israel was not simply embodied in a progressive history of salvation. Certainly it was expressed in a series of events that revealed, prefigured, or anticipated various aspects of Christ, and there was a forward dynamic in these events. Yet there was also the dynamic of wisdom in them, a kind of permanent "circling round" mystery in which the goal was more understanding of the complexity of the relation between God and man than a definitive, "linear", solution of problems this relation posed to the intellect. Reflection on the saving events both returned to what had earlier been said and saw this as pointing to what was more fully said when Christ came as the way, the truth, and the life.

Although the overarching typological relationship is between Old and New Covenants, Joseph Cardinal Ratzinger has illustrated the typological way of thinking that existed in Israel already before Christianity by pointing out that the New Moses, the Servant of the Lord of the first of the Servant Songs in Isaiah 42:1–4 (5–9), extends the message of justice, already delivered by Moses to Israel, to the peoples.[2] Here a typological movement in one sense completed within Judaism in turn looked forward to Christ, linking Old to New Covenants. To use Ratzinger's illustration, the Moses of the Torah looked forward as type to the antitype of the New Moses in Isaiah, who in turn became a type anticipating Christ as antitype.

If I can put it this way, in such typological presentation, the movement from type to antitype is not so much a progressive story of salvation as a pulsating one. The Body of Christ as it passes through history beats with a life that ties together the types and antitypes of both Old and New Testaments. This is why New and Old Testaments cannot be severed: the events of the New Testament are in some way, often in multiple ways, fulfillment of things already at least hinted at in the Old Testament. The New Testament is best understood in the context of the already existing covenantal

[2] Joseph Cardinal Ratzinger, *Turning Point for Europe? The Church in the Modern World—Assessment and Forecast*, trans. Brian McNeil (San Francisco: Ignatius Press, 1994), 71–77.

drama into which it entered. Fidelity and its testing, as one of the great themes embodying the covenantal relation between God and man, thus is recurrent in the dramas of the Old Testament.

Number 2571 elaborates one of the most pregnant of these dramas. At Mamre Abraham welcomed a mysterious Guest into his tent. The *Catechism* capitalizes the word *Guest* to show that this Old Testament story was already about the coming of Christ and the hospitality of those who receive him. Typology commonly involves what is called a spiritual sense of Scripture, and that is what we have here. The literal sense of the story is about Abraham being visited, but christologically God has written the story to be about, at the spiritual level, the coming of Christ. The coming of the Guest "foreshadows the annunciation of the true Son of the promise". That is, the annunciation of annunciations, that of Christ by Gabriel to Mary, is foreshadowed by the annunciation of a Guest, who already is Christ, to Abraham. Christ may be called "Son of the promise" because he it was who was already promised in the drama at Mamre. The "type" Father Abraham is developed in another direction in 2572. Here one of the most puzzling stories of the Jewish Scriptures, that of Abraham being asked by God to sacrifice his son, is taken as a promise of the sacrifice of Christ. What is asked of Father Abraham is like what God the Father will demand of himself.

One of the things that gives the typological drama of salvation history its texture is the fact that, as has been said, the passage from promise to fulfillment occurs all through the Old Testament and not just in the crossover from Old to New Testament. Thus no. 2574 speaks of God's covenantal promise beginning to be fulfilled in the great events of the history of Israel, in Passover, Exodus, and Law. Within Israel's history, events are related typologically, although the great typological relation is that of everything to Christ. Moses' intercessory prayer is fulfilled in "the one mediator between God and men, the man Christ Jesus" (1 Tim 2:5).

In 2576–77 Moses' "face to face" prayer is at once contemplative and intercessory. There is an old challenge, "Why pray?" meaning that if God is all powerful and all knowing, what difference could prayer make? Why should we ask for something God already knows we need? Intercessory prayer perhaps goes to the heart of this old challenge. The *Catechism* calls Moses' intercession for the people mysterious. Moses reminds God of things God presumably already knows: God is love and therefore must be righteous and faithful, God cannot contradict himself, and so on. The *Catechism* is not the proper venue for a full consideration of one of the most difficult of theological questions, but it does try to throw light on the dimensions of the problem by stressing that the relation between God and man is covenantal. If there were no cooperation of our wills with God's, if we were merely puppets or were asked by God for a kind of canine obedience, there would indeed be no need for prayer. It would at most be a way of reconciling ourselves to the inevitable, a kind of self-therapy. But the point of view of the *Catechism* is that we are truly cooperators and dialoguers with God. We talk back to the playwright. For this, God must on the one hand love us enough to seek us out and be faithful to his promises, but we also must pray that his will be done and that our mission be clarified for us.

This idea of mission, to which the *Catechism* keeps returning, needs an additional comment. In treating education in the faith, Part III of the *Catechism*, no. 2226, states, "Parents have the mission of teaching their children to pray and to discover their vocation as children of God." This is a particularly apt way of putting the question. Teaching one's children to pray could have been described as an obligation or duty, but the *Catechism* describes it as a mission. The ancient Christian tradition that parents are cocreators with God lies in the background here. To be a parent is to have a mission given by God to continue his creation, specifically in such a way that offspring will be taught to pray, that is, to recognize the Gift they are and the Creator with whom, through their parents, they are in relation, not simply as children but as children of God.

Typology is given a stunning rendition in the third paragraph of 2583. The *Catechism* notes that the prophet Elijah stood in a typological relation with Moses and that, uniquely, the New Testament brought them both forward, not just as types of Christ their antitype but as sharers in one of the greatest of the events of Christ's life, the Transfiguration. In 2576 Moses had spoken face to face with God. The place of this beholding of God was a mountain, from which Moses had to come down to address the people. Number 2583 presents Elijah as an antitype of Moses, for like Moses he beheld God, this time from a cleft in the rock. Again, before Christianity there was a "completed" typology in Judaism in which Elijah was a new, but now prophetic Moses. But Moses and Elijah were more than type and antitype and were together more than types of Christ's direct vision of God in prayer. Luke 9:30–35 places them at the Transfiguration. The types became contemporaries of him who was their antitype or fulfillment. The two Old Testament figures, who had already "seen God", stand on the mount with Jesus and speak face to face with him in his Transfiguration. They "behold the unveiled face of him whom they sought; 'the light of the knowledge of the glory of God [shines] in the face of Christ,' crucified and risen." [3]

---

[3] CCC 2583, quoting 2 Cor 4:6; cf. Lk 9:30–35.

The Transfiguration is the most striking embodiment of the notion of conversion through prayer spoken of in 2581. That the goal of prayer is conversion of heart is made "luminously clear" by Christ's Transfiguration in prayer to the Father. He is the model of what we in prayer are to become. There is a parallel implicit in the "attentiveness to the Word" of 2584. As Moses and Elijah and Christ went to the mountain to be attentive and then returned with what they had seen to others, so prayer for us is to be a conversion that witnesses to others, a going apart or into the desert that results in return with a word for others. Our mission in the world is nurtured by withdrawal from the world, by attentiveness to God in prayer.

Article 2 moves from prayer in the Old Testament to "the fullness of time", that is, the period initiated by the Incarnation, in which we live. Number 2606 speaks of "the 'today' of the Resurrection". Taking up the idea that God is a playwright, 2598 uses the striking expression "the drama of prayer" to describe Christ's time on earth as the fullest form of the drama that God had been staging and restaging since the beginning. The covenantal relation between God and man, "the drama of prayer", which had been the subject of many dramatic representations or revelations, "is fully revealed to us in the Word who became flesh and dwells among us". Christ is the Antitype, who in his prayer most clearly proclaims our relation to God. The *Catechism* draws a parallel between the burning bush and the Gospels. The burning bush and the Gospels are means by which we look upon Jesus. In the ongoing drama of prayer Jesus was already being revealed in the burning bush, and the Gospels are like that bush from the midst of which God speaks. The Gospels allow us to observe Jesus in prayer, to learn from him how to pray, and "to know how he hears our prayer".

In the fullness of time (no. 2599) Jesus reveals that prayer is filial. In the Old Testament prayer was many things, most profoundly covenantal. But the fullness of time reveals that the fullness of prayer is filial, the relation between Father and Son, and that all humanity is called to this form of prayer, that is, all are children of God. We are all "sons by adoption". In addition to all the ways the Old Testament revealed that men are related to God, which range from the awesome to the tender, Jesus in his relation of filial devotion to the Father reveals that we may approach God as our good Father. Jesus' life is a prayer or drama that lives out in our presence and for us the manner in which all are to be related to the Father. Jesus' life as a prayer is obedient unto death, and 2605 reminds us that filial prayer is crying *"Abba . . .* not my will, but yours". Number 2606 quotes Hebrews 5:7–9: "Although he was a Son, he learned obedience through what he suffered, and being made perfect, he became the source of eternal salvation to all who obey him." Number 2609 adds, "Faith is a filial adherence to God beyond what we feel and understand." Because a son learns to trust a father, he may be open with him, and 2610 says Jesus in prayer teaches us filial boldness to ask all that we need. In the Old Covenant (2614) God made many promises. In the New Covenant the great promise, revealed in Jesus, is that the Father will attend to our prayer as he attends to the Son.

Mary is so important in the drama of salvation because she is the person God had always been looking for in all the encounters of the Old Testament where he asked faith of people. She too is a great antitype. As 2618 says, "It is at the hour of the New Covenant, at the foot of the cross (cf. Jn 19:25–27), that Mary is heard as the Woman, the new Eve, the true 'Mother of all the living.' " God had always been looking for a perfect humility, for complete faith, trust, and openness, and he found them in Mary. Hence the very beautiful passage in 2617, which sums up prayer in the Christian life, "In the faith of his humble handmaid, the Gift of God found the acceptance he had awaited from the beginning of time. She whom the Almighty made 'full of grace' responds by offering her whole being: 'Behold I am the handmaid of the Lord; let it be [done] to me according to your word.' '*Fiat*': this is Christian prayer: to be wholly God's because he is wholly ours."

The mystery and drama of salvation continue to the present, centered in the liturgy taken into the individual heart (no. 2655): "In the sacramental liturgy of the Church, the mission of Christ and of the Holy Spirit proclaims, makes present, and communicates the mystery of salvation, which is continued in the heart that prays." The drama of salvation continues in the present in the heart that prays. All through Part IV, the *Catechism* shows how salvation history bore or carried with it the development of prayer. This story does not close with the New Testament and the Lord's Prayer, but continues to the present. It is Church history's heart. From the Jesus Prayer of the ancient Church, to the retreat into the desert of the Benedictines, to the return to the city of the Franciscans and Dominicans, to the development of an incarnational prayer committed to the conversion of the world by the Jesuits, to Vatican II's concern that the whole people of God be a praying people, each epoch and historical situation in seeking prayer suitable to itself has discovered new aspects of what it is to pray. Still, to say that the drama of salvation continues in the heart that prays the sacramental liturgy is to see the heart of history being played out in the going forth of the liturgy from Jerusalem that begins in the Last Supper and Pentecost.

Irresistibly this calls to mind the book noted above in Chapter Two, by Jean Leclercq, who chronicled some of the detail of the medieval monastic moment of the drama of salvation.[4] For the monk liturgy was the continuation of salvation history, of the redemptive act, into the present. Without necessarily leaving their monasteries, the followers of Saint Benedict saw themselves as participating in the spread of the gospel, for above all in the Mass Christ was being brought to the nations. In embracing the sacraments, peoples new to Christianity joined their histories to God's saving acts. Missionaries might literally preach the Gospel, but wherever Christ was present on the altar, the drama of salvation continued. The Eucharist is always offered today, and the covenant drama of prayer plays in our hearts.

The earlier sections of Part IV of the *Catechism* have much to say of the drama of salvation as it affects every human being. As it nears its close, the *Catechism* increasingly addresses the individual. What it had centered in the call of type to antitype earlier it increasingly centers on the fact that today the drama of salvation is taking place in each of us (no. 2807): "[W]e are immersed in the innermost mystery of his Godhead and the drama of the salvation of our humanity." The Kingdom is today (no. 2816): "The Kingdom of God has been coming since the Last Supper and, in the Eucharist, it is in our midst." The Eucharist becomes the summation of the drama of salvation, Christ in our midst now.

---

[4] *The Love of Learning and the Desire for God: A Study of Monastic Culture*, trans. Catharine Misrahi, 3rd ed. (New York: Fordham University Press, 1982), 194–96.

INDEX